Grace
SIMPLY
Grace

Dealing with Condemnation and
Legalism in the Christian Life

Grace
SIMPLY
Grace

*Dealing with Condemnation and
Legalism in the Christian Life*

Ron Smith & Rob Penner

YWAM Publishing
A Ministry of Youth With A Mission
P.O. Box 55787, Seattle, WA 98155

Grace...Simply Grace

Table of Contents

Part Five

The Practice of Grace: Free to be Servants

Part Six

Conclusion: The Ultimate Act of Grace

Appendix

Thirty Minutes a Day

Introduction

The Legalist

Legalism is a time bomb waiting to explode, hidden inside a nicely wrapped package. Though others may admire such fine wrapping, it's only a matter of time until the package shatters and the legalist is left sitting in the ruins of burnout and condemnation. Most churches have their share of legalists, and it is likely that most Christians are part legalist themselves. Let's consider the following two people to better understand the heart of a legalist.

The "bomb" inside Betty, a lady in her early twenties, has been threatening to detonate for several years. To everyone else, Betty is as reliable as Mother Teresa, as dedicated to Christ as one can be. Her parents can always count on her to be good, her friends look to her when a need arises, and her pastor knows she will participate in every church function.

But no matter how much Betty does, she always feels she's not doing enough, because she also feels that somehow she isn't quite pleasing God. This haunting sense of God's disapproval drives her from Bible study to prayer group, from buying each "New and Improved System for Personal Devotions" at her local Christian bookstore and joining every church outreach program to standing at every opportunity to recommit her life to Christ. In spite of her "gold-medal performance" as a Christian, Betty continues to feel that God considers her a failure.

James is a young man with a different set of problems, the greatest one being lust. Though he has never actually committed fornication, James struggles continually with impure thoughts. He lives in dread that his Christian friends will discover what is happening inside his brain.

Attached to this mental impurity is a sense of deep shame, a shame that permeates his feelings about himself and his position before God. James has determined many times to discipline his mind, to think on "whatever is pure," to stop eyeing pretty girls when they walk by—but he just can't seem to help himself!

Betty and James are composites of various people with whom we have all spoken. They sit next to us in our church pews, they are our Sunday school students or teachers, they are the missionaries we support. But an even more disturbing thought is that they are hidden within the consciousness of each of us who confesses both Adam and Christ as his parents. Betty and James are legalists, people who feel that they are either superior Christians because of their fine moral standards or many good deeds, or that they are inferior, always falling short of God's approval.

In the first-century days of the New Testament Church, Christians would deviate from correct doctrine and practice in one of two ways. Firstly, they abused the grace of God by not living holy lives, by continuing to indulge in the fleshly living of their immoral past. In his first epistle, John wrote to a church infiltrated by teachers who were telling the believers that they could sin as much as they wanted. The church at Corinth also seems to have struggled with this problem of licentiousness.

But the second and greater problem in the New Testament Church was legalism. Paul was the pioneer spokesman for the message of God's free grace through Christ, and this simple theme underscored all his writings. He preached this message with power (I Cor. 1:17,18) and through it, saw demonstrations of the Spirit (I Cor. 2:1-5). He stated that this message of God's grace through Christ is the means of growth (Col. 2:6,7) and that the grace of God develops Christian character (Titus 2:11,12). He believed that this plain truth was enough to unite a divided people (Eph. 2:8-16) and that everything else in life was useless in its light (Phil. 3:3-11). In fact, God considered Paul's heartbeat message important enough to make him author of nearly half (13) of the 27 New Testament books.

His letter to the Galatian churches was devoted to this subject of God's grace given freely through Christ. In these pages, Paul called the legalist into a theological boxing ring and dealt a resounding series of knockout punches. Though this letter was written more than 1,900 years ago in a culture far different from ours, its message is timeless. We have written this book in an attempt to make the message of Galatians clear to Christians in the twentieth century—those who do not find circumcision or the Law of Moses to be issues in their Christian lives.

History gives us examples of those who have legalistically sought to make themselves worthy Christians. The apostle Peter stopped eating with Gentiles in the first century. Some centuries later, a monk named Benedict attempted to conquer his lust by rolling around on thorn branches on snowy winter days. Still later, Martin Luther tried to find God's approval through fasting and self-inflicted physical torture. These were all people who loved God and desperately wanted to please Him.

Legalism remains in our boxing rings of Christian faith and ethics. It attacks us with condemning questions, then obliges by giving the response:

Have I prayed enough?—*No!*

Have I tithed enough?—*No!*

Is God angry with me because I missed church? —*Of course!*

Paul showed that such questions do not usually find their source in God, because His call is to relationship rather than increased activities. Through Galatians, we are given tools that will help us defeat legalism and condemnation in our Christian lives. "For freedom Christ has set us free; stand fast therefore, and do not submit again to a yoke of slavery" (Gal. 5:1).

Part One

Background:
The Attack on Grace

1

How to Pervert the Pure Gospel

Scripture is timeless. Like no other book, the Bible aptly speaks to contemporary issues, though it was completed about 1,900 years ago! This age-old best seller is in a class of its own.

College or high school textbooks are revised every few years to fit changing needs in education. Moreover, the bookstore in your local shopping mall sells books far different from those of your parents' day. But the Bible, life's most important "textbook," remains unchanged.

Paul's letter to the Galatians, penned about 50 AD, summed up an important theme of Scripture: by His grace alone, God saves man. This simple message has left a permanent imprint on history. In the sixteenth century, Martin Luther meditated on this old, old letter, and then helped to shake a corrupt church from its legalistic spell. Through Galatians, he understood the truth of the Gospel, and the world has never been the same.

The message in Galatians should still be reforming the Church. More specifically, it should be transforming our Christian experience. Every tendency toward righteousness by works will be shattered as we contemplate the timeless truth of Christ's *finished work* on the Cross. A.W. Tozer has said that the Cross will cut into our lives, bringing selfishness to an end. At that point, we will be able to establish new patterns in living new lives.

Setting for the Story

Before we study the message of Galatians, it's important to understand the reason it was written. If we can identify the problem in the Galatian church, perhaps we'll see similar problems in our own lives. If that's the case, then Paul's letter will have been written to us as well as to them. Let's look first at Paul's initial audience.

Galatia, a province of the old Roman Empire, was situated in the heart of what we know as modern Turkey. Paul, on his first missionary journey (Acts 13,14), had visited four of the region's southern cities.

In each of these places Paul's message received a similar response: the Gentiles accepted it and the Jews rejected it. The Jews not only were unresponsive, but became violently jealous as Paul's message grew in popularity among Gentiles. At one point, they were so infuriated that they nearly stoned the apostle to death.

How could a preacher instill such hateful passion in his audience? This will become clear as we study Paul's message in Galatians. For now, we will simply say that Paul preached a message that didn't fit with the Jewish concept of righteousness through works.

In spite of such perilous persecution, Paul left Galatia having established some solid Christian fellowships. Following a short visit to his home base (Syrian Antioch), he traveled to Jerusalem to share exciting testimonies of Gentiles being set free by Christ.

At the same time, however, Judaizing Christians (almost a contradictory term) began bringing a perverted version of the Gospel to these liberated babes in Christ. Judaizers held firmly to the Law of Moses, believing that salvation rested in one's ability to meet its standards. They taught that these new Christians must be circumcised—an old Jewish religious ritual. We'll look more at this ritual later. (From now on, we will refer to this group as the "circumcision party.")

Their "gospel" came with a few extras. It stressed man's work in salvation, rather than God's. It was tangible, attractive, seductive. A child would have difficulty refusing it. Young Christians would have difficulty discerning its error. Let's observe the circumcision party's message. It may be more familiar than we'd expect.

Nine Methods of Gospel Perversion

Through Paul's letter, we are given information on at least nine false claims made by the circumcision party. These Gospel-perverters of Galatia had some pretty convincing arguments for their own brand of "Christianity." It wasn't long before the immature babes in Christ had swallowed their neat little appeals.

1. "We aren't ones to drop names, but we do come from some very important people" (1:1; 2:12).

Paul's opening claim described his own ministry. He was "an apostle—not from men nor through man..." (1:1). This stood in contrast to the false teachers' claims that they had a mission from the head church. (In 2:12, Paul referred to those who supposedly came from James, pastor of the church in Jerusalem.)

Name-dropping is often used to gain popularity. A pastor friend recently had some trouble in his church with three strangers. They just showed up one Sunday and began "prophesying" in the middle of the service. Since the message didn't seem "weird," a few weeks passed without confrontation. But by the third or fourth Sunday, these strangers had virtually taken over the service with their "prophecies." It was now time to confront.

The pastor grabbed a few elders and sat down with the strangers. They found that these three had been "ministering" in the area at several well-known and respected churches. Some big names were mentioned which would aid their popularity. Well, with a few quick calls, the pastor learned that these people did "minister" at several churches, but not because they had itinerant ministries. The truth was that no church would permit them to continue speaking for more than a Sunday or two.

James was the "big gun" of the first century church. Making him their leader could open wide doors of ministry for the circumcision party, no matter how corrupt their group was. Christians would be unwittingly swept away in a sea of false teaching, following man rather than God. But we know from Acts 15 that James did not really send them out. It was a big hoax so they could be accepted. False teachers are usually more concerned with acceptance from man than with pleasing God.

2. "We come from a fine line of chosen people" (3:7).

The circumcision party emphasized their "rich heritage." As far as they were concerned, Abraham, the father of faith, had himself been saved by being circumcised. Therefore, good sons of Abraham would do as their ancestor did. Right? Wrong!

True, Abraham had been circumcised, but that physical act merely symbolized a heart dependent on God. His real "children" share the attitude of faith that shaped his life. Counterfeit sons of Abraham share only the outward symbols of religion.

God has no grandchildren. No one can ride into heaven on the coattails of someone else. Personal faith in God through the finished work of Jesus is the only road to eternal life.

So far, we've observed two lies the circumcision party told about themselves. Now we'll continue to study their "ministry" by observing four lies they told about Paul.

3. "Your favorite teacher doesn't even believe that any more" (5:11).

In order to have a receptive audience, they had to really stretch the truth about the Galatian church's founding father. According to them, Paul himself had rethought the "grace" message, and had decided to change back to a "circumcision" emphasis. Imagine the impact this lie would have on the undiscerning babes in Christ who had respected Paul as their spiritual father.

Of course, Paul quickly denied this tall tale. Moreover, he said that even if he did change his message, they shouldn't believe him. Rather, they must hold fast to the simple truth already received.

By now, we should be seeing that the issue of who teaches what is relatively unimportant. The simple Gospel of Jesus is not subject to change by anyone, be he a big-name preacher or an average Joe Christian.

History provides us with countless sad examples of people changing the Gospel. The Mormons, Jehovah's Witnesses, and Children of God are a few contemporary examples. Each of these groups consist of people who have followed not the Gospel itself, but a teacher who changed the Gospel.

4. "You know, the guy who taught you this stuff had some definite problems" (1:10).

A message may best be destroyed by questioning the speaker's credibility. The false teachers of Galatia knew this tactic well. Their argument would have gone something like this: "Paul is a man-pleaser. He taught this silly little grace message in order to not offend anyone. Of course, he realized all the work it takes to know God. He was just too afraid of your rejection to tell you."

Paul pointed out the absurdity of this lie in verse ten. Men-pleasers and God-pleasers are like oil and water: they can't be mixed. Paul had suffered persecution because of his grace message. To him, this proved that he had lived, and still did, a life of trying to please God rather than men (5:11). After all, men-pleasers find the Cross much too heavy to carry.

5. "Do you know what Paul really did after he was saved?" (1:20).

In relating his travels to the Galatians, Paul assured them he wasn't lying. His bit of defensiveness indicated that false teachers had cast doubts on his own testimony.

Three years following his conversion, he went to visit Cephas (Peter) and James in Jerusalem. At that time, he would have shared his testimony with these church leaders. They, in turn, had acknowledged his genuine experience with the Lord.

The circumcision party denied that Paul ever met with Cephas and James. Had he visited these leaders, the "grace message" would certainly not have been preached in public. Such good Jews as Cephas and James would have stamped out the smoldering flames of such an abominable heresy, wouldn't they?

Wrong again, boys! Paul went to great lengths to stress his interaction with Jerusalem's church leaders. At one point, he even had to oppose Cephas—the "rock"—for not living out the Gospel of grace (Gal. 2:11).

False teachers will discredit the testimony of even a true messenger of God. Remember when the Jews brought Jesus before Pilate? They implied that this "revolutionary" was trying to overthrow the Roman Empire (Luke 23:2). Here the Jews followed their pattern for doing away with uncomfortable teaching: get rid of the teacher.

6. "Sorry to break this to you, but your old teacher forgot you existed" (4:12-19).

Paul reminded his children in Christ of the "good old days" when they first became acquainted. The bond which held them together then continued to tug at his heart. Concern for their well-being in Christ ranked high on his list of priorities. Paul referred to them as "my little children." Could a more endearing term possibly be used? He longed for the true image of Christ to be formed in their lives.

The circumcision party used this shepherd-flock relationship as another target for attack. By attempting to remove every vestige of Paul's authority from the church, these manipulators thought they would be free to assume their own chain of command.

False teaching results in a divided church. The wicked heart of man can never hope to achieve true unity. Only the Gospel—Christ's redemptive work on the Cross—can change man's heart and open the door for undivided fellowship. This is why Christian apologists are so important to the church. Many refer to them as "witch hunters." Often seen as cruel, unfeeling people who cause division, most Christian apologists are actually great unity seekers. To them, unity is based on truth and can only take place around the Cross of Christ.

We have looked at lies which the circumcision party told about themselves and about Paul. This section now concludes with three other attempts at stealing the pure Gospel.

7. "We just need to make a few little changes in what you believe" (1:7).

The false teachers of Galatia attempted to "pervert" the Gospel. Pervert is a strong word, but may also be understood by the word *change*. The entire problem in Galatia can be summed up in four words: people changed the Gospel. As far as Paul was concerned, no more heinous crime could be committed.

The finished work of Christ is just that—finished work. No additions or deductions are allowed. Such simplicity has continually been rejected by the Church. Two thousand years of church history have seen "Christians" trying to add to or subtract from the simple Gospel of Christ's work on the cross. It has never worked.

Most heresies are not conscious efforts to make the Gospel better. Most heretics don't view Christ's work on the cross with the critical eye of an editor for his writer's work. The motive of a Gospel-perverter is often a desire to be made more acceptable to God.

The great preacher Andrew Murray presented a challenge to Christians to accept Christ's finished work as complete, explaining that our worthiness is not in ourselves or in our consecration but in Christ Jesus.

8. "Now, they don't teach this 'grace' message in the head church" (4:25-26).

The circumcision party taught the Galatians to submit to the Jerusalem church. To the Jewish mind, Jerusalem was "where it all happened," the place where God and man met together. Paul countered that line with a bold statement of his own: Jerusalem is in bondage. God, the Creator of heaven and earth, receives no big thrill from a physical city, but He does love the spiritual community. Christians relate to a spiritual Jerusalem, the universal Church. (We'll look more closely at this term later.)

People can easily be impressed by large, fancy churches or prominent seminaries. Or we may have our ears tickled by popular speakers and writers who promote dramatic church trends. These are minute in light of God's huge work accomplished through the death of Jesus. God's people, awestruck by mere names, need to scrutinize themselves and return to the simple emphasis of Christ and the Cross.

9. "My, what fine disciples you are. Have you tithed yet this month?" (4:17)

This final point deals more with motive than an actual lie. The circumcision party "made much of" the Galatian believers, doting over them like a money-hungry young woman on a rich, old man. What was the goal of their flattery? Earning a nice, fat bank account. Scripture warns about those who "flatter for gain" (Jude 16). The false teachers in Galatia didn't really care about the people they were teaching. They mostly wanted to receive something.

A true Gospel teacher wants to give of his knowledge more than he wants to receive. True, the workman is worthy of his wages, but to the one who works for the Gospel, monetary gain is secondary. True reward is fulfillment gained from serving the Giver of all good gifts.

The similarities between the war waged on the Gospel of grace in Galatia over 1,900 years ago and the problems in today's Church are almost eerie. The message of God's saving grace as preached by Paul received attacks by some of the original Gospel-perverters. Dress them up in twentieth-century attire, and we'll see that they continue to live on, still attacking the Gospel of grace.

Simplicity may seem out of place in our complex world. Man's knowledge is growing at an alarming rate. The computer of five years ago is tremendously outdated. Trendy philosophies of previous decades have given way to more "progressive" ideas. Why not throw the Gospel into the human progress machine and "adapt" it to fit twentieth-century man?

The answer is: people cannot change history or mankind's condition. The death of Jesus on the Cross and His subsequent resurrection stand as the focal point in human history. That truth can never be altered. A response will always be asked of us. Paul's letter to the Galatians gives a timeless response to Gospel-perversion. The simple Gospel is the key to all Christian living. To alter it brings the opposite—death. It's as simple as that.

Part Two

The Receiving of Grace: Starting with Simplicity

2

Greetings from Two Authors

*Paul an apostle—not from men nor through man,
but through Jesus Christ and God the Father, who
raised him from the dead—and all the brethren who are
with me, to the churches of Galatia:*

*Grace to you and peace from God the Father and
our Lord Jesus Christ, who gave himself for our sins to
deliver us from the present evil age, according to the
will of our God and Father; to whom be the glory for
ever and ever. Amen.*

Galatians 1:1-5

Galatians begins with the name of Paul, its author.
However, the first five verses reveal anything but a self-
centered emphasis. God the Father is mentioned five
times (three references by name, two by pronouns) and
Jesus Christ five times (two by name, three by pronouns).
We are about to read a God-centered, God-inspired plea
for the simple Gospel.

Best sellers are seldom written by unknown authors.
Paul was careful to emphasize his own authorship at the
outset of this short letter. His very name would command
respect, calling otherwise disinterested ears to perk up
attentively. In underlining his authorship of Galatians,
Paul moved past a desire to bask in the limelight of

respect. He pointed to another Author: the Originator of grace, peace, and even of Paul himself. God is the ultimate Author, His signature indelibly inscribed on all His finished work.

The finished work of Christ begins this epistle. Paul stressed the *resurrection* of Jesus as he identified himself (v. 1). He lives because Jesus lives. The *death* of Jesus is emphasized as blessings are invoked from God (vv. 3,4). The atoning death of Christ is the fountainhead of God's blessings. Jesus is central to the book of Galatians, and to life itself.

Now we are ready to look a little more closely at the two authors of Galatians: Paul, the author of the letter, and God, the Author of everything.

Paul, Author of the Letter

Today's letters almost always close with warm greetings and a mention of the author's name. The reverse was true of letter writing in Paul's day. In the first century, a letter normally began with identification of the author, then make mention of an intended audience, and finally give warm greetings to that audience. Once these essential courtesies were out of the way, the author could get down to business.

Paul was eager to emphasize that *he* was writing this letter. Charged by the circumcision party of undergoing a theology-shift, the apostle wanted to leave no room for mistake. He *had* preached the simple Gospel of grace, he *was then* preaching it, and God forbid he should ever deviate from it.

Names are important because reputations are usually attached to them. We are all known for something. Some people are known for their sense of humor, some for their social concern, some for their sharp tongues. Paul had a reputation for preaching "salvation by grace." The circumcision party polluted Paul's name by heaping unfounded accusations upon him. Here in this love letter of rebuke, Paul was forced to defend his own name, as well as the Gospel he preached.

Now let's look at the source of Paul's ministry. The word *apostle* means "one who is sent out." Obviously, behind everything sent is a sender. As in this case, the identity of the sender is of paramount importance.

Imagine you serve as your nation's ambassador to Russia. You have a very important summit meeting with the Russian Premier regarding nuclear weapons. After three days of dialogue, you mention that your own President did not order or sanction these meetings. Rather, the ambassador from some obscure nation sent you to meet with the Russian Premier. What kind of response would you receive? You might as well have said, "My wife sent me here."

In declaring the source of his ministry, Paul was careful to mention that man is *not* the source. The circumcision party seemed to thrive on saying they were sent by James. To them, the name "James" would serve as their ticket into the hearts of these unsuspecting babes in Christ. Paul had one up on them, though. His mission was from the very Gospel-maker Himself: God, in the persons of the Father and the Son. A call and commission from God was Paul's only claim to ministry. Without it, he had no authority to preach the Gospel.

His initial call is explained in Acts 9:1-16. God first gave Paul a glimpse of his purpose in ministry during his conversion experience. Years later, Paul and Barnabas were sent on their first missionary journey by the Holy Spirit's command (Acts 13:2-4). True, men did lay hands on them and sanction the rightness of their ministry, but ultimately their call came from God.

In the middle of explaining his credentials, the apostle mentioned that God raised Jesus from the dead. Now why would Paul explain his ministry's source, and then throw in a seemingly unrelated statement about the Resurrection? What is the significance of the resurrection of Christ in relation to Paul's apostolic calling?

Paul's non-fictional experience with the risen Lord Jesus proved to be both terrifying and life-changing. The book of Acts records his testimony of the encounter three times. Seeing the resurrected Jesus—the One he had persecuted—devastated Paul and dramatically changed his life. The risen Jesus was the source of Paul's ministry.

Now that he had clarified the source of his ministry, Paul mentioned the fact that he had a team (v. 2). In most of his letters, he listed several brothers or sisters by name: both those he was with and those he was addressing. Strangely enough, in his letter to the Galatians, Paul made no statement about his location or about the identity of his co-workers.

No one can say for sure the names of the brethren with Paul. They probably included either Barnabas or Silas. Whoever they were, Paul made another point about his ministry: people were with him in it. He was not out on his own, preaching some abstract Gospel that God revealed to him, that only he understood and believed. He was a team-worker. The members of his team preached the exact same Gospel. To that end, this love letter of rebuke (paradoxical, but true) was as much from Paul's co-workers as from Paul himself.

God, Author of Everything (1:3-5)

Now we come to the real Author of Galatians. That is not meant to merely be a statement about the inspiration of Scripture. Rather, by stating God's authorship of Galatians, we are emphasizing that He is the true source of its message.

Galatians is about grace—God's unmerited favor given freely to man. God's grace is the reason for our salvation, and is man's only lifeline in a sea of deadly sin.

The Author of all grace and peace has revealed Himself to man through the Person of Jesus. In the words "Grace to you and peace from God the Father and our Lord Jesus Christ," Paul identified the ultimate Author of Galatians. The One who met Paul with the message of grace was the One who met the Galatian Christians with the same message. Without Him, there would be no letter.

"Grace to you and peace from God...." was the standard opening line of Paul's epistles. We might call it his trademark. An understanding of God alone as the source of salvation shaped Paul's thinking. He is forever remembered as the one who realized his utter wretchedness apart from the grace of God. His life message has been shouted loudly through more than 1,900 years of history.

As was the case in all his writings, Paul also referred to God the Father and the Lord Jesus Christ in this initial greeting. As a rule *God* generally refers to the Father, while *Lord* is most often used in reference to Jesus Christ.

The term *Lord* in the New Testament corresponds to *Yahweh* in the Old. It is a statement about the deity of Christ; He is Master, King, supreme above all else. The word *Jesus* is the Greek form of the Hebrew word *Yeshua*. It means "Savior or Deliverer." *Christ* is the Greek translation of the Hebrew word *Messiah,* meaning "Anointed One," that is, One anointed by God for a specific purpose. Put them all together and we arrive at a good definition for "Lord Jesus Christ": the Supreme Deliverer, anointed by God for salvation. Here again is the simple Gospel seen in the name of Jesus.

Now that we have considered the Person of Jesus, we can look at the description of His work. Jesus is the One who "gave himself for our sins." Sounds like a return to third-grade Sunday school, but if our emphasis ever moves from this truth, we may as well abandon our faith. That simple, one-time sacrifice of Christ is central to our ongoing Christian experience.

"Giving himself for our sins" speaks of a priestly work accomplished by Jesus. In Old Testament Judaism, priests offered animal sacrifices on behalf of the people. An innocent lamb, goat, or bull would be brought to the priest. One slice of a sharp knife through its throat would do away with every vestige of life. The victim was then hacked to pieces and mounted upon a large, square altar where it would be burned as an offering to God.

This helpless, innocent animal became a substitute for the sinful offender, who deserved death for his own sin. Jesus, "who gave *himself* for our sins," *is* the ultimate and complete sacrifice. No more animals need be slain for us; the perfect sacrificial Lamb has been slain. No working or choosing can make us acceptable to God, except choosing to exercise faith in Christ (which faith is also a gift from God). Simple faith in Christ's finished work on our behalf is our only grounds for acceptance by God.

The work of deliverance wrought by Jesus on the Cross has very specific objectives. Deliverance always refers to salvation from a bad situation. Many children's stories are based on the plot of a hero prince delivering some damsel in distress. In the same way, our own Prince of Peace has rescued us from the greatest distress—an eternal future in hell—and has given us a new heaven-bound life.

Jesus has removed us from the influence of the present evil age to be with Him forever. This may seem hard to comprehend or believe. Sometimes the present evil age weighs upon us heavier than ever. It's important that we come to a good understanding of the term *present evil age*.

First-century Jews believed they were living in the present evil age. To them this would change at the Messiah's coming. His appearance would mark the beginning of the "age to come." Paul spoke in his writings of these two ages in the same breath: "...he raised him from the dead and made him sit at his right hand in the heavenly places, far above all rule and authority and power and dominion, and above every name that is named, not only in this age but also in that which is to come" (Eph. 1:20,21). He, along with other New Testament writers, modified popular understanding of the coming of God's kingdom. They taught that although we live in a corrupt and corrupting world, God's kingdom has broken through.

The initial victory of God's kingdom on earth took place at Calvary. Jesus' death has set us free from the *power* of sin. However, we are not completely free from the *affects* of sin until the final return of Christ. Adam's fall into sin continues to blemish our world and our Christian lives. Death and sickness still occur. Christ has not given us a "paradise on earth," try as we might to make paradise a reality.

At the same time, the death of Christ has given believers great earthly benefits. In Ephesians we read about being "sealed with the promised Holy Spirit, which is the guarantee of our inheritance until we acquire possession of it...." The Holy Spirit is a type of "down payment" for the big payoff to come at Christ's return.

Imagine having a kind boss who would give advances on your paycheck. Whenever you were short of money during the month, you could merely ask and he'd come through with the help. The advance would tide you over until payday, when you would receive the full payment.

We are living in the days of down payment. The day will come when the advance on our paycheck won't be necessary. We will receive all. The New Testament is full of references to the hope of Christ's return.

That is the future for any serious Christian. Earthly desires for a career, a family, or worldly success are minuscule in light of our hope of Christ's return. (See the following diagram.)

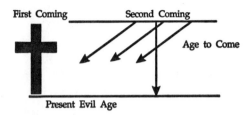

Our understanding of position and possession in Christ will affect the way we live. If one believes that he has in Christ everything he'll ever get, he completely denies that he can be touched by sickness, poverty, sin, or even death. He believes that the completion of Christ's work has perfected every part of his being. Neither will he allow room for moral imperfections in himself or others. His attitude will be something like, "I'm redeemed; I'm clean; sickness and sin will not be seen."

On the other hand, the one who knows he's only received a portion (though a very generous one) lives in expectation of something more. The portion received is more than sufficient to cover all needs during his stay on earth. And the hope of God's coming kingdom will carry him through difficult times of failure and confusion.

This should answer some of the questions that we as Christians may ask. For example, "Why was Mrs. Jones healed of cancer, but not me?" Or possibly a more common question, "Why do I continue to have anger toward people if Jesus has cleansed me from sin?" Certainly God is a merciful, healing Father with power to spare over sickness and sin. However, as long as we are Adam's descendants, the effects of Adam's sin will not be completely eradicated.

Romans tells us that all creation is groaning to be delivered from the bondage of Adam's sin (Rom. 8:22,23). We are part of that creation. Thanks to God, we know deliverance from the power of sin through Jesus. And through the same Jesus, we wait eagerly for the final coming of God's kingdom, our full release from the effects of sin.

History had seen the team of mankind beaten by its opponent—sin. Then two thousand years ago, man's Star Player showed up. Jesus stepped into the game and won the victory for man. Now we are waiting for the Star Player to return and collect His trophy. That will be the time for a complete victory celebration. Sin will be completely defeated once and for all.

All of this is done for the glory of God. The true Gospel is God-centered. God does not save man because of his works, right choices, strengths, or abilities. God's grace alone is the reason for salvation, and He alone deserves the glory. We are delivered from this present evil age when God is gracious to deliver us. Unto Him alone be glory, majesty, dominion, and honor.

This first paragraph from the letter to the Galatians concludes with a well-known Christian word: *Amen.* Related to the Hebrew word for truth, some use the term to say "let it be" or "so be it." At times, the word *amen* also found use in Hebrew as an acrostic for this phrase: "The Lord Our God is Faithful." May our eyes be always drawn to the faithfulness of God, our Savior, Redeemer, and Hope.

3

New is Not Always Better

I am astonished that you are so quickly deserting him who called you in the grace of Christ and turning to a different gospel—not that there is another gospel, but there are some who trouble you and want to pervert the gospel of Christ. But even if we, or an angel from heaven, should preach to you a gospel contrary to that which we preached to you, let him be accursed. As we have said before, so now I say again, if any one is preaching to you a gospel contrary to that which you received, let him be accursed.

Am I now seeking the favor of men, or of God? Or am I trying to please men? If I were still pleasing men, I should not be a servant of Christ.

Galatians 1:6-10

The 1970s will be remembered as the "me decade." During those post-hippie years, Western culture became comfortable with all kinds of new things: easy divorce, free love, legal abortions, and so on. New values and lifestyles replaced older traditional beliefs, and society has never been the same. Few Christians would say that these new improvements have actually made life better.

The church at Galatia faced a similar problem, only much more than values was at stake. The simple Gospel, the actual root of values, had come under attack. To the Galatians, the new Gospel would seem very much like the one Paul had preached, with a few improvements. As Western culture has met with a sad fate for discarding traditional values (sexual diseases and troubled families are two examples) , so the Galatians would be the losers for "improving" on the Gospel.

Paul was astonished that they could so swiftly forget that which saved their lives (v. 6). *Astonished* is the same word used in the gospels to describe people's response to the miracles of Jesus. With the same kind of amazement, Paul could hardly believe what he was hearing. How could those who had actually experienced God turn their backs on Him?

The Galatians' sin reveals a sad human weakness: forgetfulness. Many Christians suffer from a spiritual Alzheimer's disease; that is, we can very quickly forget God's grace. One may have known a spectacular miracle of God yesterday, and tomorrow become involved in utter sin. Today's valley often obscures the memories of yesterday's sunny mountaintop.

Remember how the children of Israel sinned with the golden calf (Ex. 32)? They had known remarkable deliverance from Egypt—plagues that destroyed the enemy, a parted sea, and so on. They then viewed God's glory on the mountain before falling into new depths of sin. Their new idol resembled familiar Egyptian images, and they attributed salvation to it.

We read this story and think, "How could they be so stupid? No one in their right mind is that forgetful!" True, their unfaithfulness seems to border on mental instability, but let's examine ourselves before pronouncing judgment on them. Every Christian in the world is prone to unfaithfulness. May we view Israel's fickleness with the old response: "There but for the grace of God go I."

Notice what the Galatians deserted by rejecting the

Gospel preached to them (v. 6). Paul's main charge against them wasn't "doctrinal error" or "mistaken ideas." Rather, they had abandoned the Person of God by entertaining these new ideas. God is at the heart of the Gospel message. Every little deviation from the true Gospel is a step farther away from God Himself.

Many Christians today feel that theology is unimportant. Seminaries are jokingly referred to as "cemeteries." True, the relegation of Christian living to mere facts and head knowledge should be argued against, but the term *theology* actually refers to the study of Christian beliefs. True and pure doctrine is essential to our Christian lives. False doctrine removes us from strong relationship with God and from accurate Christian experience.

Think about a new marriage. What if the wife decides one day that the idea of marriage is wrong? She loves her husband, but can't live in the institution of marriage anymore. She packs her bags and moves back to her parents' home. Has she merely left an idea? Of course we would say that the young wife has deserted not only the institution of marriage, but also her husband.

In embracing a doctrine of "works = righteousness," the Galatians were leaving the One they had married. Consider the story of the good Samaritan. Would it have made sense for the injured man to pledge allegiance to the priest or Levite who had rejected him? Surely he would be indebted to the kind Samaritan who had shown him mercy.

The contrasting elements of that story are similar to the ones in this letter. The Law is that which pointed out our wickedness. As we lay naked along the road of sin, it passed us by, robed in its garb of moral perfection, not lifting a finger to help in our distress. God, on the other hand, is like the good Samaritan. Stepping from His own elevated position, He graciously reaches out and pulls us from the place of despair. Clothing us with His righteous-

ness, He meets every need. Would it make sense to turn
back to that cold, impersonal, uncaring Law that left us
naked and alone? That is precisely what the Galatians
were doing: rejecting the One who had accepted them,
and accepting the one who had rejected them.

How had they rejected God? By denying His message
to them. Paul explained that the Galatians had been
"called in the grace of Christ" (v. 6). He didn't say that
they were asked to do works for Christ. The grace of God
had reached out and removed them from the present evil
age. Only He was the reason for their salvation. They had
been helpless, unable to do anything that would make
them acceptable to God. This grace is commonly termed
"unmerited favor."

You may have heard the phrase for which the word
grace serves as an acronym:

God's
Riches
At
Christ's
Expense.

All the goodness of God has been poured out on man
through the Person and Work of Jesus. Thoughts of righteousness through acts of our own will are filthy stains on
the spotless garment of God's grace.

God has taken initiative and given the method for
saving man. To emphasize our response over and above
God's completed work is like congratulating the one who
drank the milk instead of the farmer who worked for it.
God alone is worthy of honor for the work He has done.
Redeemed man deserves no glory for being saved.

The book of Acts shows how the Galatians had been
called "in the grace of Christ." Paul and Barnabas were
the Gospel carriers to Galatia, preaching God's Word to
both Jews and Gentiles. The Jews stirred up controversy

and poisoned the minds of unknowing Gentiles. In one Galatian town, Iconium, they weren't able to drive the apostles out, much less stop the Holy Spirit's activity (Acts 14:3). God confirmed the Gospel of grace by granting signs and wonders through the apostles' ministry.

In Lystra, Paul and Barnabas again stirred up quite a commotion (Acts 14:8-22). The religious inhabitants there believed that the gods had once visited their fair town, but that the people had failed to show them adequate hospitality. Therefore, the townsfolk made a vow that if the gods ever returned, honor would certainly be given them. When Paul healed the lame man, it was naturally assumed that the gods had decided to pay another visit. Out came the high priest of Zeus to offer a sacrifice to Paul (Zeus incarnate!). Of course, Paul declined the honor and attempted to preach the Gospel to these mistaken Galatians.

Nearby circumcision party members, jealous of the success of these Christian missionaries, quickly came to refute Paul's teaching. Gathering the people of Lystra to their side, they stoned Paul and dragged him out of the city to die. Undaunted, the apostle got up, reentered the city, left the next day, and returned after a short time away. That's the type of calling the Galatians began with: a call from God, confirmed both by miracles and a witness of endurance under persecution. Paul was shocked that they could reject something made so plain to them.

Furthermore, they rejected it for a "different gospel." Not content to let God hold the entire responsibility to save man, the Galatians wanted to initiate salvation for themselves. The word *different* is the root for our English word *heterodox*, which refers to any teaching opposed to established doctrine. The Galatians had traded the saving grace of Christ for something completely different.

Different is not the only adjective used to describe this new Gospel. Paul went on to say that this Gospel was contrary in nature to the true Good News (vv. 8,9). As we progress through Galatians, we will see that this new message differed in both source and method. To the Galatians, it appeared to be an improvement on Paul's Gospel. In actual fact, this new Gospel was very different and could be compared to the difference between unleaded and leaded gasoline. If one keeps putting leaded fuel into an engine designed for unleaded, the motor will eventually be destroyed.

Our modern church is inundated with different gospels (and that doesn't mean Matthew, Mark, Luke, and John). Someone placed a poster on a billboard recently, advertising his "true" church, "The Church of Universal Brotherhood." It seems that this group had discovered some ancient documents hidden in the Vatican that told "what really happened at Calvary." Jesus had actually lived through the Crucifixion and had gone somewhere to form the "true" church. Of course, this church propagates a much superior gospel, because it allows every human being to respond to his religious instincts in whichever way he feels most comfortable.

Most Christians have no problem discerning such teaching as heresy. But more attractive and subtle forms of false teaching do exist; teachings that aren't necessarily wrong in themselves but present an incorrect emphasis of Christ's Gospel. Any doctrine which highlights the work of man—faith, choices, holiness, unity—must not be emphasized over and above the work of Christ. The Cross of Jesus must remain central. We cannot move from it, beside it, past it, or around it.

The world's religions are seeing a huge push toward syncretism in the twentieth century. Syncretism is a combination of religious beliefs aimed at promoting unity. The Hindu Gandhi is extolled as a godly man by some Christians. Use of Eastern religious thought is finding a comfortable place in sermons and pastoral counseling.

The Church is called upon to unite with those of other religious persuasions. At what cost?

Unity with non-Christian philosophies and religions will result in a dimming of the true Gospel. We see the Coca-Cola singers from all around the globe joining hands, singing about world peace and love. They appear so humanistically nice. But the simple Gospel of Christ's death for man is the only acceptable basis for true unity to the Christian. (Remember, we are discussing faith, not politics or social services.) Unity for the Christian Body is drawn from the Head, Christ. Any other unity has no appropriate head, and is therefore mindless.

Our attention now turns to the problem-makers. They were described by Paul as ones who are "troubling" the young believers (v. 7). James, pastor at the Jerusalem church, also referred to some with a penchant for causing trouble (Acts 15:24). Whether or not Paul and James referred to the same group, both were comprised of those who destroy the very foundations of the true Gospel.

The troublers were probably not foul-mouthed, intimidating terrorists, holding the Galatians at gunpoint until they changed their beliefs. Heresy is seldom so obvious. The circumcision party was most likely comprised of nice, friendly people who flashed inviting smiles and kissed babies. Their message probably stressed "the blessings of obedience" while they painted mental images of God's little acre of utopia. No matter how sweet their personalities, or how delightfully they tickled ears, these Judaizers were troublemakers.

How did they make trouble? By perverting the pure Gospel of Christ's finished work. Now, a false teacher is not our usual concept of a pervert. That word usually gives the image of a child molester or a rapist, someone with a sick, abusive, sensual tendency. Maybe we should think of the one who tampers with mankind's only ticket from hell to safety as an even worse pervert. The one clouding God's message to man with man-centered ideas is guilty of the worst perversion ever.

The preacher's name and background are relatively unimportant. What matters most is his emphasis: God or a system. Paul didn't leave room for his own team, or even heavenly messengers, to alter God's complete communication through Jesus (v. 8).

Common Jewish belief held that angels delivered the Law to Moses. The circumcision party taught that since this was the case, the Law had to be the superior revelation. They assumed that they had something to add to the Gospel. Little did they know that their sin had brought them under a curse.

The Greek word for curse, *anathema*, has also crept into our English language. It is a very strong word, to be used in the sense of utterly condemning someone or something. The concept has an Old Testament partner. On entering the Promised Land, the children of Israel were to bring God's judgment against the wicked Canaanite tribes, totally destroying every vestige of them. They were labeled for destruction because of their wickedness. An *anathema* was pronounced upon them.

Jesus gives us a similar picture in the New Testament. Anyone who causes a young babe in Christ to sin may also expect a fearful end. It would be better to have a millstone tied around his neck (we might say "be fitted with concrete shoes") and be cast into the sea (Luke 17:2).

The consequences of leading someone away from his only hope are frightening. The curse is greater for the heretic because he is not merely playing with a private little sin—others are being affected by it.

An Old Testament prophet once gave a man-made message to another prophet, claiming angelic inspiration. The listening prophet believed the lie, and it caused his death (I Kings 13). In more recent times, Jim Jones claimed a heavenly origin for his message and ministry. He led hundreds to their deaths in South America.

Position, reputation, charisma, charm, and experience—these are trash if the pure Gospel is not being preached. Martin Luther fought against powerful church leaders who were acclaimed as infallible by many. Their power did not impress this German monk who viewed only God's complete communication as infallible. May our hearts be so ablaze with a fire for the Gospel that any perversion (large or small) of a Christ-centered emphasis would be consumed in the fire of truth.

This isn't a license for fault-finding or criticism. Many preachers and teachers have made and will make mistakes by handling the word of truth inaccurately. They must be approached, corrected, and restored with a spirit of gentleness. But in our love, let's be careful not to smooth over the error and discard the simple Gospel that man is dying to hear.

Now where does the curse come from? The swift repetition which Paul made here (vv. 8,9) was taken directly from the Law of Moses. Later in this letter, Paul gave a short summary from a list of curses found in Deuteronomy 27:15-26 (Gal. 3:10). He was probably reflecting on this passage as he penned these statements.

He did not become emotionally upset, shake his finger, and say, "Well, curses on you if you don't believe this!" Rather, he was making a statement based on the Law itself: preachers of the Law are under a curse, because they can not possibly live up to the Law (see Gal. 6:12,13). He was merely stating a fact. The Law cannot save; it can only serve as the guiding light to hell. The Law is the dispensation of death to any who would place their trust in it.

Salvation by the Law reminds me of the story about the poor, struggling, college lad who wanted to marry his rich girlfriend. Deeply in love, they would certainly marry, except for one small matter—the girl's parents. As part of "high society," their daughter must marry someone from another wealthy family. The college boy could do everything right but would never gain their approval. He is condemned without being given a chance.

The Law is like the girl's parents, condemning the sinner who wants to have fellowship with God. Its standards are too high for anyone. No person can fully meet its requirements. We are driven to God as sinners, casting ourselves upon His grace for salvation. He alone is given credit for that.

Legalists would think this grace business makes salvation too easy, that we need to do a few things to help out the salvation process. Work-oriented man loves to hear such talk about self-righteousness. He doesn't like to picture himself floundering helplessly in sin, unable to control his own destiny. Not exactly an ego-booster, is it? Thinking we can actually determine our own fate helps us to straighten our ties and hold our heads up high. After all, God wants us to have some self-respect, doesn't He? We can easily confuse self-respect with self-righteousness, which is comparable to filthy rags (Is. 64:6). Paul did not mince words. A curse was pronounced on anyone who preached a man-centered Gospel.

It takes courage to stand up for the simple Gospel of grace. Paul had been accused of the opposite: preaching grace with a motive of pleasing man (v. 10). Fearing man is probably the best way to pervert the Gospel.

A recent movie told of a congregation who had long been served by a people-pleasing senior priest who would only talk about nice things, happy times, and blessings. A young intern, who preached a fiery, uncomfortable message, was sent to the church to be trained. Whenever the young priest said something the congregation found uncomfortable, a chorus of throat-clearing and coughing drowned out the sermon.

The one who preaches the true and simple Christ-centered Gospel will continue in spite of throat-clearing. Paul rebuked the circumcision party by pronouncing a curse upon them. The fear of man did not hinder him from promoting the simple Gospel of grace. More than desiring popularity, Paul desired that these beloved people understand the source of their hope. They needed Jesus much more than Paul needed popularity.

Questions, Review, and Interpretation

1. Who preached the Gospel to the Galatians first? What was the basic content of his message?

2. Who upset the Galatians' faith? How?

3. How has the "present evil age" been combined with the "age to come"?

4. How were the Galatians deserting God? Consider what "deserting God" means in a practical way.

5. Look up the word *anathema* in a dictionary. Why does Paul pronounce this curse upon false teachers?

Application:

1. Consider the fact that you live in the "present evil age," though the "age to come" is upon you. What are some ways that these two ages conflict in your Christian life?

2. What are some teachings you have heard that seem to be contrary to the message of God's grace through Christ?

3. How have you deserted God? What aspects of the Gospel do you seem to easily "forget"? What should you do to not desert God?

4. How has the Gospel been perverted in either your past or present sphere of Christian relationships?

5. What practical things can you do to keep the Cross of Christ central?

Part Three

The Testimony of Grace: An Apostle's Story

4

The Calling of a Criminal

For I would have you know, brethren, that the gospel which was preached by me is not man's gospel. For I did not receive it from man, nor was I taught it, but it came through a revelation of Jesus Christ. For you have heard of my former life in Judaism, how I persecuted the church of God violently and tried to destroy it; and I advanced in Judaism beyond many of my own age among my people, so extremely zealous was I for the traditions of my fathers. But when he who had set me apart before I was born, and had called me through his grace, was pleased to reveal his Son to me, in order that I might preach him among the Gentiles, I did not confer with flesh and blood, nor did I go up to Jerusalem to those who were apostles before me, but I went away into Arabia; and again I returned to Damascus.

Then after three years I went up to Jerusalem to visit Cephas, and remained with him fifteen days. But I saw none of the other apostles except James the Lord's brother. (In what I am writing to you, before God, I do not lie!) Then I went into the regions of Syria and Cilicia. And I was still not known by sight to the churches of Christ in Judea; they only heard it said, "He

*who once persecuted us is now preaching the faith he
once tried to destroy." And they glorified God because
of me.*

Galatians 1:11-24

So far we have heard Paul's siren, sounded to warn of
a wicked crime called Gospel-perversion. By this point,
the Galatians—along with us—realized the simple Gospel message delivered by Paul was not subject to change.
From here through the rest of his letter, Paul backed up
the truth of this claim.

He wrote from three angles: his own *testimony* of grace
in the first two chapters; the *history* of grace in chapters
three and four; and the *practice* of grace in the final two
chapters. We'll begin by observing how God's powerful,
saving grace turned a criminal into one of the greatest
Christian witnesses of all time.

We've entitled this chapter "The Calling of a Criminal," because that was how Paul viewed himself. A hero
in man's eyes, he came to see that his sinful pride was an
abomination to God. This passage in Galatians outlines
his movement from destructive sinner to redeemed saint.

In verses 11 and 12, he summarized his testimony,
showing why Gospel perversion repulsed him the way it
did. "For I would have you know, brethren, that the
gospel which was preached by me is not man's gospel.
For I did not receive it from man, nor was I taught it, but
it came through a revelation of Jesus Christ." Echoing a
statement from verse one about his apostolic ministry,
Paul claimed an unearthly source for his message. He
didn't learn his Gospel in a "Friends of Jesus" Bible study.
He learned it from Jesus Himself.

Anyone can make a statement, build a doctrine, or
start a church by adding the words "God told me" to his
ministry. How was Paul different? Who's to say he was
not just another mystic, preaching some fanciful illumina-
tion? After all, Muhammed and Joseph Smith both ranked

themselves as "prophets," enlightened by "God" through revelation.

Paul's experience differed from these by three words. At the end of verse 12, he claimed his message came through a "revelation of Jesus Christ." Had he merely said, "My message came through a revelation," period, we might very well be suspicious. But Paul's experience brought him face to face with Jesus Himself, God's greatest means of communication (Heb. 1:1-3). The apostle didn't ask the Galatians to follow some mystical visionary. Rather, he compelled them to receive God's revelation in the true-to-life person of Jesus.

When Jesus came to earth, he fulfilled God's plan for the ages (Eph. 1:4-10). In the Old Testament, we see God revealing Himself to various saints, showing them the way of salvation. Moreover, throughout these instances of revelation, verse after verse points to the Messiah.

Bible scholar J. Barton Payne lists over 3,000 verses from the Old Testament that point to Jesus, God's ultimate Word to this world. (See *Encyclopedia of Biblical Prophecy*, J. Barton Payne, Harper and Row, 1973, p. 680.) The revelation given to Paul simply confirmed Christ's divine ministry. Paul was not creating a new religious system; he was gaining insight into God's age-old plan of salvation through the factual, historic, "it-really-happened" ministry of Jesus.

Christians have a bad habit of following fallible people. Sadly enough, today's enthusiastic church loves to follow exciting men with "God-told-me" ministries. Following these people and their vision is not the problem. God has always given leaders to the Church. The problems arise when a vision or "word from God" becomes an object of worship, removing one's focus from a Christ-centered life. The exciting "new word" has then replaced God's complete revelation through Jesus.

Imagine you are a youth pastor with a dynamic ministry in your church. Seeing your contagious Christian life, your young flock respects and almost reveres you. For some time, you have felt a burden for missions and have faithfully shared this with the group. Because of your charismatic personality and their desire to serve God, the youth group begins a fantastic missions program. Committees are formed, projects launched, funds raised, workers sent. Pancake sales, car washes, and prayer teams are organized. The kids begin to eat, drink, and sleep missions. Great! Right?

Well...maybe. Missions are great; the more support the better. But when a program overshadows the work of Christ, the very *reason* for missions becomes obscure. The Gospel of Jesus slips into second place behind a "good" work. And it all began with a word from God.

Does this mean that God doesn't speak to individuals anymore, that we only hear Him through the Bible? Of course, God still speaks to people in a multitude of ways. But daily, experiential revelations must never distract us from simple faith in His complete revelation: Jesus. The Person and Work of Christ was, is, and will always be a Christian's focal point.

Paul's statements about revelation are important, not because they prove God still speaks to people, but because they offer a personal testimony of the Gospel of Christ. This sinner-turned-preacher understood the Gospel as God revealed it. Truth does not evolve, undergoing changes or receiving additions by spiritual mystics. The old message becomes new when a sinner grasps its truth and it becomes his own life-transforming word.

So, what is revelation? It's a difficult term to define in one sentence, but let's put it down as this: *God's historic communication from Himself about Himself to man.*

Historic, because it progressed from creation to Christ.

Communication, because God has spoken in a clear way that all men can understand.

From Himself, because God is the source of all saving knowledge.

About Himself, because God alone is able to save.

To man, because man is the object of God's saving work.

Does someone reading in a dimly lit room hold the paper up to the light switch? Of course not. Paul didn't attempt to teach the Galatians how to have faith in *his* revelation. He fully realized his own role as God's light switch. Rather, through his experience, he points to the Author of all revelation, the source of all light. Paul's own encounter with the Light merely confirmed that Christ is God's message to man.

Let's bear this in mind as we study Paul's testimony in Galatians 1:13-17. He wrote about three stages in his salvation: an anti-Christian former life (vv. 13,14), a clear conversion experience (vv. 15-17), and confirmation by a nod of approval from Peter and James (vv. 18-24). This passage highlights the pivotal moment in Paul's Christian experience and his entire life: a revelation of Jesus.

Paul's "former manner of life" (vv. 13,14) shouted volumes of proof for God's saving grace. He described himself as one determined to annihilate the Church. Zeal for God's chosen race and revealed religion prompted him to show no mercy toward "fanatical, heretical" Christians. His love for Judaism painted him as the most "able" son of God, the greatest legalist. All this combined to make him (as he said in another letter) the greatest of all sinners (I Tim. 1:15).

The Galatians had heard of Paul's life before he met Jesus. He had probably given his testimony during his visit with them. Paul seemed to enjoy telling about God's saving grace. Repeating it twice in Acts (Acts 22,26), he also wrote it unashamedly to the Philippians (Phil. 3:4-6). Not proud of his wickedness, he pointed out his sin to draw attention to God's grace.

As far as Paul was concerned, life in Judaism went hand in hand with life in sin. As Israel's national religion, Judaism was based on the Law of Moses (the first five books of the Bible). Many Jews came to believe that salvation could be earned by keeping the Law, which initially included everything from not committing adultery to not eating pork. In time, they created all kinds of trivial laws, adding those to the Law of Moses and oppressing its adherents with them. A successful Judaizer couldn't take 2,000 steps from home on the Sabbath, or eat without washing the sinful world from his hands.

By making the Law God's standard for salvation, Judaizers elevated one aspect of revelation above God Himself (like the youth pastor with the good missions program). The Law became their focal point; keeping its requirements, their life's mission. God, on His heavenly scale, would weigh good works against evil deeds. If the Law-keepers managed to tip this scale in their favor, they could expect many temporal and eternal blessings in return. Judaism, as Paul knew it, exalted man. Man kept the Law, man won the prize. God could be called a robot, forced to act upon the basis of someone's works. Paul, the most zealous of all Judaizers, received quite a shock when he began to see God's true nature.

In Philippians, Paul said he was blameless in regard to legal righteousness (Phil. 3:6). Yet he spoke of this "blamelessness" in connection with his life of sin (see Titus 3:1-4). God views man's self-righteousness in the same way a hygienist views sewer water. Paul came to see that his self-righteousness was very foul to God. He found the source of true righteousness: it comes from God, through Christ.

Violence played a key role in Paul's quest to become "legalist of the century." The Bible makes no effort to be kind when describing his heresy-hunting crusades. He used violence in trying to destroy the Church (Gal. 1:13);

he ravaged the Church, dragging off men and women (Acts 8:3); and he breathed threats and murder against the Lord's disciples (Acts 9:1). Paul persecuted the Way to the death (Acts 22:4), punished them in raging fury (Acts 26:10), and persecuted with zeal (Phil. 3:6). As described here before his conversion, Paul is not exactly the kind of guy we'd welcome into our Bible study!

Paul is not portrayed as a desperate truth-seeker who exhausted every avenue in a frantic search for fulfillment. He figured he was already living right, and that God owed him a nice reward for such fine zeal. With works unequaled by the strictest Pharisee, he confidently added righteousness to self-righteousness. Put in simple terms, Paul was self-sufficient.

Not just a complacent synagogue-sitter, he also felt an unsurpassed zeal for the traditions of his fathers (v. 14). The Chinese word for *zeal* literally means "hot heart." This sums up Paul's heart for Judaism; he was a man consumed with passion for the Law. Doubts about the rightness of Judaism never entered his mind. Advancing beyond his peers as an extremely capable Pharisee, Paul felt he lived in the center of God's will.

The New Testament often repeats the story of Paul's life of obstinate sin, painting a striking picture of God's unmerited favor. God came to a sinner who was not seeking, and proved His own saving grace. Through *His* power and mercy alone, God yanked Paul from the hell-bound bus called "self-righteousness." Paul assumed he had cut a clear path to heaven. Instead, he would come to understand the true destiny of "works = righteousness."

Why so much emphasis on Paul's stiff neck? Shouldn't we highlight his deliverance rather than his sin? We certainly should, but the more we understand sin's magnitude, the better we'll acknowledge the depth of Christ's work. As Paul grew to learn his own depravity, so must we recognize the horror of our sinful hearts. May

God remind us of the ugliness that only He can beautify, the filthiness that only He can purify, and the crookedness that only He can straighten.

God's salvation of a non-seeker speaks clearly about His grace. But more than that, it fills us with hope for anyone. The one who tames the lion can certainly tame the small wildcat. If God could reach Paul, a self-righteous Jew with no perceived needs, He can by all means reach those we love and pray for. The first key to salvation is revelation from God.

Now for the most important words of Paul's life: *But when He*. These words mark the beginning of an entirely new creation. We've observed the violent legalist walking down a crooked road. The phrase "but when He" acted as Paul's turning point from hell's highway to the "straight and narrow" way leading to eternal life. *But* should be the pivotal word in every Christian's life. Even if the word doesn't appear in our testimonies, the "but God" concept begins every true salvation experience. Let's look at some Old Testament examples:

Abraham lived in paganism, but God....

Moses was a murderer on the run, but God....

Gideon grew up in idol worship, but God....

Isaiah saw his own sin, but God....

Though often used to begin our excuses, the word *but* is often used in Scripture to show contrast. Look at Ephesians 2:1-6. In the first three verses Paul made some sad observations about man's lost condition: we were dead through sins, followed the prince of the power of the air, lived in the passions of our flesh, and so on. Then, in verse four, he wrote the pivotal words of change:

"*But God*, who is rich in mercy, out of the great love with which he loved us, even when we were dead through our trespasses, made us alive together with Christ...." May our own "but God" always be remembered as the lifeline thrown to a drowning sinner.

Paul referred to God as "he who had set me apart before I was born" (v. 15). The omniscient God planned Paul's salvation before his parents knew whether they'd have a girl or boy. Jeremiah mentioned that God called him from before birth, as well. Salvation is not our own good idea. We don't walk through years of sin and then decide we'd like to "try God to see if that works." God specially calls all His people, based on knowledge that He alone possesses.

Is God surprised by the salvation of a sinner? Heaven does rejoice, but it doesn't throw a surprise party. God didn't wipe His brow after Paul's conversion and say, "Whew, I didn't think he'd make it." His great plans for Paul didn't change when He saw what an evil person Paul had become. God waited and waited and waited. Salvation comes from Him, on His time schedule.

This doesn't mean we act like department store dummies, waiting for God to put us in the salvation window. Of course we respond to God's initiative of grace. But that response must never overshadow God's initiative. With humble hearts bowed in submission, we cry out to God for the very ability to respond.

Salvation is God's idea, His brainchild. We should always give Him credit, never overemphasizing our "right choice." Do I get credit for using the telephone which Alexander Graham Bell invented? Is my wisdom applauded for using the electricity discovered by Benjamin Franklin? Is it even worth mentioning that I responded to God's miraculous, saving grace?

Paul was "called through his grace" (v. 15). He didn't say "God called me through my faith." God's kindness served as the only reason for Paul's salvation.

Faith, one of God's gifts to us, continues to play a part in the Christian life as we trust God for such things as guidance, insight, and healing. These things are possible when a Christian exercises faith that God exists, and is

consistent with His character and word. His promises will
be fulfilled as we put our trust in Him and fulfill the
conditions He's given us.

You may have heard the chair illustration used to
describe faith. The one who sits on the chair wins no
medals for his great faith in the chair. The chair holds him
up; people remark on its fine quality. The same is true in
the grace /faith relationship. Jesus is God's ultimate communication with man. After years of shouting his own
good works to God, Paul finally heard God's message:
Jesus. This wasn't what the killer of Christians expected.

We've heard the story about Paul traveling down the
Damascus road, flaunting death warrants for Christ's
disciples. Then, from nowhere, blinding lights dashed
him to the ground, and God spoke. There lay a man,
wholeheartedly intent on destroying God's work, receiving a revelation of God, from God. He didn't make the
right choice or pray the right prayer. He was granted new
life by a Name he had endeavored to vanquish.

What a contrast to one who spends years in the lotus
position, trying to find his karma. Or one who piles up
good works in order to come back a rich man rather than
a termite in the next life. Or one who continually does
good Christian works to keep a handle on God's blessing.
We are saved by grace, because God revealed Jesus to us.

We often hear about Christians who manage to "find
God," as if He were the lost sheep. They view salvation
from a backward perspective. We don't find God; He
finds us marching down our own Damascus road. May
we be grateful to the search party that sought us out as
we drifted through the blackened forest of sin.

Paul did not "confer with flesh and blood" after this
experience (v. 16). He didn't search for man's stamp of
approval on God's work. The term "flesh and blood" is
an Aramaic term meaning "people." Paul received a revelation independent from man. God alone had shone a

light into Paul's dark life. Jesus had appeared to him, and in Jesus, he found salvation. Paul's vision led him into a three-year term of self-inflicted solitary confinement, alone with God in the Arabian desert. Here, he really got to know the One of whom a mere glimpse had brought blindness.

The question still remains, "Can we trust anyone's revelation if they put the name of Jesus on it?" Remember Joseph Smith; he put Jesus' name on his "revelation," and misguided millions of people, who became Mormons. Experience itself may not be trusted. It must be scrutinized in light of the historical Jesus.

For Paul, this meant a visit with the apostles in Jerusalem. Although not needing their approval, he respected their positions as ones who had walked with Jesus. Was the Jesus he saw the same One they knew? His short visit with Peter and James confirmed a valid experience with God. The Jesus they knew during His earthly ministry had become known by one independent of that ministry.

For us, this means that we should compare our "revelations" with Scripture (especially the New Testament, but not ignoring the Old Testament). Then we confirm it with trusted Christian friends and obey what the Lord told us to do in the revelation.

The Christians who had been subject to Paul's persecution could rejoice (v. 24). A dramatic turnaround in Paul's life pointed to God Himself. They didn't glorify Paul's willpower; they glorified God, the One holding salvation's keys. The finished Work of Christ, life-changing for them, had gotten through to another sinner. Glory to God!

5

Traveling for the Truth

Then after fourteen years I went up again to Jerusalem with Barnabas, taking Titus along with me. I went up by revelation; and I laid before them (but privately before those who were of repute) the gospel which I preach among the Gentiles, lest somehow I should be running or had run in vain. But even Titus, who was with me, was not compelled to be circumcised, though he was a Greek. But because of false brethren secretly brought in, who slipped in to spy out our freedom which we have in Christ Jesus, that they might bring us into bondage—to them we did not yield submission even for a moment, that the truth of the gospel might be preserved for you. And from those who were reputed to be something (what they were makes no difference to me; God shows no partiality)—those, I say, who were of repute added nothing to me; but on the contrary, when they saw that I had been entrusted with the gospel to the uncircumcised, just as Peter had been entrusted with the gospel to the circumcised (for he who worked through Peter for the mission to the circumcised worked through me also for the Gentiles), and when they perceived the grace that was given to me, James and Cephas and John, who were reputed to be pillars,

gave to me and Barnabas the right hand of fellowship,
that we should go to the Gentiles and they to the
circumcised; only they would have us remember the
poor, which very thing I was eager to do.

Galatians 2:1-10

Truth and love are great motivators. Love for the truth, a combination of the two, has won many battles. Our foremost heroes, both fictional and real, distinguish themselves by fighting for truth and justice. Depending on literary leanings, names like Perry Mason, Joan of Arc, and Superman come to mind.

Paul's frightening vision and subsequent blindness left no doubt in his mind about the truth of the Gospel. He traveled far to preach its saving power and defend its claims. His missionary service is recorded in the book of Acts. This passage in Galatians reveals an apostle's persistent effort to keep the simple Gospel just that—simple.

By explaining such labors of love for Gospel truth, Paul hoped to provide further support for his message. He was now off to Jerusalem for a visit with Peter, James, and John, the three noted pillars of the Early Church. We'll see that the Gospel wasn't just a nice bedtime story for Paul to tell his children, or to have framed and hung on his kitchen wall. Its vital importance led him to travel far, oppose heretics, and stand up to big names.

This paragraph in Galatians resembles an episode recorded in Acts 15. Many Bible scholars believe that the two passages offer different accounts of the same story. Three groups of people are highlighted, giving us an interesting courtroom drama:

- The defendants (or the "good guys"): Paul and his friends—defenders of truth.

- The plaintiffs (or the "bad guys"): the circumcision party—Gospel thieves.

- The mediators (unbiased judges): Peter, James, and

John—leaders of the Jerusalem church.

This gathering was commonly referred to as the "Jerusalem Council," but we'll call it the "Jerusalem Trial." Paul, together with God's message of salvation, was on trial as the defendant. The plaintiffs, better known as the circumcision party, accused Paul of Gospel-perversion, attempting to conceal their own criminal identities. A landmark ruling was made in this court, one which has affected Christians ever since, including ourselves.

Paul received a subpoena for court appearance from God Himself. He went up to Jerusalem "by revelation" (v. 2). The same word is used for this type of revelation in chapter one, but now with a different emphasis. Earlier, we read that Paul's conversion process was begun by revelation. However, his conversion didn't make God crawl back into His hole, satisfied that He had opened another sinner's eyes. Revelation is an ongoing process, and God had just begun to work in Paul's life. Paul's journey through life became a supernatural experience, daily being led by God. Such guidance is a Christian's privilege, something that shouldn't be ignored.

Fourteen years earlier, Paul's experience (and message) had received approval from those in Jerusalem. However, attacks on the Gospel had persisted, and so did Paul's rebuttals. A study of his New Testament letters reveals a man continually trying to preserve the simple truth of Christ. Assaults on the Gospel have continued for more than 1,900 years, and still persist today. Will we have Paul-like hearts, going to great lengths to protect the simple truth?

An important witness for the defense traveled with Paul to appear in court. Titus, an uncircumcised Gentile, came to testify of God's saving grace (on behalf of non-Jews). You may have heard it said that no better proof for the Gospel exists than a transformed life. Scripture doesn't tell us about Titus' background, but we know he later became a leader in the first-century church. He was a prime example of God's grace made available to all.

At the Jerusalem Trial, the real issue became apparent: circumcision. This little bit of surgery marked the Jews as God's Covenant People. Any Jewish proselyte must be circumcised to enter into that divine covenant. God first revealed this ritual to Abraham at the founding of the Jewish nation (Gen. 17). Originally meant to symbolize a heart dedicated to God, Jews had made circumcision a basis of salvation. Only through the knife could someone have true fellowship with God.

Paul combated this mentality in the New Testament by explaining that true circumcision is a matter of the heart, not the body (Rom. 2:28,29). That is, true circumcision removes the foreskin of the heart, that which blinds man from seeing his Creator. Whereas Jews required Gentiles to be circumcised as a pledge to the Law, Paul presented a new answer to legal righteousness. Man is justified through Jesus, not good works. Through Christ, the Gospel is available to all people. Jewish laws became mere ethics.

Imagine you are a Western missionary, sent out by a church in which all members take Sunday afternoon naps. On your mission to Africa, you see a tremendous revival take place in a certain tribe. This particular group of natives loves to go swimming on Sunday afternoon, but you explain that if they really want to follow God, they must take Sunday afternoon naps. You have imposed your church's culture on this tribe, and thereby tarnished the Gospel.

This may seem a ridiculous example, but by propagating circumcision, the Jews were doing the same thing. Cultural surgery became a salvation requirement. Paul vehemently opposed this type of thinking, knowing that "Jesus + anything" is not a Gospel formula.

Of course, the Jerusalem Council decided against circumcising Titus. Their verdict confirms the Gospel's truth, highlighting the fact that it stands alone, unmarked by man's good ideas.

You may be wondering what happened to the plaintiffs' case. It wasn't mentioned because their argument was so weak. However, even weak arguments can destroy the truth if left unopposed. Paul went on to say how he handled his opponents at (or "under") law.

Like many who destroy the Gospel, the circumcision party flashed a "churchy" image. Probably fluent in "Christianese," they quickly gained acceptance from most of the brethren. Few recognized the unchanged, wicked hearts which lay beneath their external righteousness. Only one so acquainted with, and grounded in, the simple Gospel could expose such heresy.

Paul labeled them "false brethren" (v. 4) in the same way we would refer to phony paintings. Usually, forgeries are difficult to spot because they appear so real. An art expert, however, has no trouble distinguishing them; he can pick out phony paintings at a glance. In the same way, the apostle who knew the Christ-centered Gospel so well could easily spot a false brother.

These imitation Christians had many of the common Christian markings, but lacked the most important element: grace. Their relationship with God depended on deeds they had done rather than on the deed Christ had done. Beginning with circumcision, they dutifully worked their way into God's field of blessing.

A true Christian starts out in a state of helplessness, unable to do anything worthy of God's favor. As the blood of Jesus cleanses him and the Holy Spirit indwells him, he begins the Christian walk. Rather than waving his good works in God's face, he recognizes that God's saving grace is now the only reason for his righteousness.

This should encourage us as we approach God. Have

you ever come to God in prayer, feeling unworthy to be in His presence because you failed to read your Bible for a few days? Or maybe you made a wrong choice, and you think God must be very upset? That's circumcision party Christianity. There's only one reason we can approach God: Jesus died and prepared a way for us to the throne of grace. Bible reading or making "right moral choices" are works that do not tear the curtain separating us from God's presence.

Paul and his cohorts did not yield to the false brethren (v. 5), but stood firm upon Gospel ground. Not only did they travel for the truth, they also stayed put for the truth. Here is another aspect in our defense of the Gospel: standing firm against assaults.

Subtle pushes to warp the simple message of Jesus are often felt by Christians. Society isn't comfortable with something that stands out on its own, appearing to make elevated claims. It's okay to believe the Gospel as long as we maintain the status quo and accept the philosophies of others. If someone preaches a different emphasis than Jesus—well, that's just their ministry. We may be told to respect the "anointing" which God has given them.

Somehow Paul couldn't make himself respect heresy. Were he active in our twentieth-century church, he would certainly be labeled "divisive." (Actually, one of Paul's major themes in his letters is unity.) What may appear as divisiveness in Paul's letters had a very specific goal: Gospel preservation for those who need it (v. 5). Like a lifeboat, the Gospel is salvation for passengers on the sinking ship called "worldly existence." By silencing the circumcision party, Paul prevented them from poking holes in and deflating the Gospel lifeboat. His life mission kept him afloat, continually searching for drowning people. Had the circumcision party prevailed, many lives would have been lost.

Keeping sight of man's lost condition is essential in

our fight to keep the Gospel simple. We aren't battling for a pet doctrine but for people's eternal destinies. The message of the 1970s song "What the World Needs Now is Love, Sweet Love" has permeated society. True, the world does need love, but not the type of "love" we know today. From the view of a humanist, love causes us to accept anyone and anything, branding any negative thought as hurtful.

By acting from this mindset, we will love people into an eternal fire. Jeremiah preached a true message about God's wrath over Israel's sin, and most of his audience shrugged him off as "just being negative." Instead, they embraced a fairy-tale type of message, closed their eyes to the reality of their own sin, and hoped for the best. They perished.

Thank God for Paul, who fought for the Gospel that it might be preserved for us. Certainly we will thank him when we meet him in heaven. Will anyone be thanking us for waging war against anti-Gospel teachings?

"Those of repute added nothing to him" (v. 6). These include the three pillars of Jerusalem's church: Peter, James, and John. Human reputations didn't impress Paul. Several years back, he had gotten a glimpse of Someone else. Seeing God had somehow dampened the appeal of big names and spectacular ministries.

More than four centuries ago, an "insubordinate" monk walked in those same steps. Martin Luther came to grips with the enormity of Christ's Work done on his behalf. This revelation of Jesus dramatically changed him, and lowered his opinion of corrupt church hierarchy. He subsequently began to vehemently oppose them for the sake of the Gospel. As with Paul, a revelation of God had lessened Luther's fear of man.

Gideon is another example of this. The son of an idol worshiper, Gideon was timid and afraid until God appeared to him. But once he saw the Lord, this once fearful young man contended against God's enemies. He destroyed his family's idols, and fought against and defeated those who oppressed God's people. A revelation of the Almighty God resulted in a de-exaltation of man.

This doesn't mean that Paul became disrespectful toward Peter, James, and John. He held them in high regard, or he'd never have bothered to visit them. After all, the same Jesus who had chosen him had also chosen them. Paul certainly valued their judgments and respected their ministries.

Paul's time with the three men highlighted four aspects of his relationship with them:

- They added nothing to his message (v. 6). The Gospel of Jesus that saved them was not subject to change.

- They recognized Paul's unique ministry (v. 7). God called Paul to minister to Gentiles. Peter had been called to the "circumcised." Those "circumcised" who "do all the right things" need God as much as anyone.

- They supported and identified with Paul's ministry (v. 9).

- They encouraged Paul to minister to the poor (v. 10).

A common complaint against the Gospel of grace is that it produces irresponsible people, ones who say a prayer and try to coast into heaven. Actually, the Gospel of God's grace served as the basis for Paul's good works. Grace inspired, motivated, and enabled him to work for others.

Paul left Jerusalem having accomplished his purpose. The simple Gospel which he had preached was confirmed as true. Those who tampered with it were labeled "false brethren," ignorant of Christian freedom. The battle was over, but as we'll see in the next chapter, it would be fought again. The next time, the Gospel offender would be a true brother in the Lord.

6

Guess Who's Coming to Dinner?

But when Cephas came to Antioch I opposed him to his face, because he stood condemned. For before certain men came from James, he ate with the Gentiles; but when they came he drew back and separated himself, fearing the circumcision party. And with him the rest of the Jews acted insincerely, so that even Barnabas was carried away by their insincerity. But when I saw that they were not straightforward about the truth of the gospel, I said to Cephas before them all, "If you, though a Jew, live like a Gentile and not like a Jew, how can you compel the Gentiles to live like Jews?" We ourselves, who are Jews by birth and not Gentile sinners, yet who know that a man is not justified by works of the law but through faith in Jesus Christ, even we have believed in Christ Jesus, in order to be justified by faith in Christ, and not by works of the law, because by works of the law shall no one be justified. But if, in our endeavor to be justified in Christ, we ourselves were found to be sinners, is Christ then an agent of sin? Certainly not! But if I build up again those things which I tore down, then I prove myself a transgressor. For I through the law died to the law, that I might live to God. I have been crucified with Christ; it is no longer

*I who live, but Christ who lives in me; and the life I now
live in the flesh I live by faith in the Son of God, who
loved me and gave himself for me. I do not nullify the
grace of God; for if justification were through the law,
then Christ died to no purpose.*

Galatians 2:11-21

During the racially tense sixties, the movie "Guess
Who's Coming to Dinner?" began playing in American
theaters. Sidney Poitier starred as a black man who was
visiting for the first time his prospective white in-laws.
His girlfriend had told her parents to expect a young man
for dinner, but decided to leave the color of his skin as a
surprise. Their reactions to the prospect of a black son-in-
law flashed the prejudices of many Americans on the
silver screen.

We've given this chapter the same title, because Peter
reflected the attitudes of the bigoted parents. Rather than
stain his reputation by eating with "those awful Gentiles,"
he turned his back on them. Jews of social status would
look with disdain upon one who mingled with such
common people.

Jews had very low opinions of non-Jews, expressing
their sentiments through very demeaning names. *Dogs,
pigs,* and *sinners* are examples of words used to describe
the "unchosen many." The Jewish mentality ran something like this: "We are God's elect, and you aren't. If you
want to join the exclusive 'Covenant Club,' you will need
to rise to our standards. Circumcision is a definite must,
as are other ceremonial laws. Keep these, and we just may
accept you as a member. If not, well...you'll have to find
others to dine with."

Throughout history, a meal has often served as the
best place for fellowship. As visitors to your church are
made to feel welcome by an invitation to dinner, so people
in the first century expressed hospitality by sharing a
common meal. In refusing to eat with Gentiles, the pious

Jews conveyed a clear message: Gentiles are substandard.

So here Peter found himself in a difficult situation, having to choose between accepting the Gentiles or being accepted by fellow Jews. Some of the "Covenant Club's" more significant members were coming to town, and they just might take away his membership card. Unfortunately, he made the wrong decision and rejected the uncircumcised Gentiles. Although he gained the Jews' acceptance, he faced the wrath of Paul. But the issue was much more important than hurt feelings. By rejecting people who look only to God's grace for salvation, Peter had rejected the entire Gospel message.

By failing to share the common meal, the Jews actually made a statement about circumcision. Gentiles would be recognized as true brethren and God's elect only when the Law became their standard. Paul argued the absurdity of this claim, and again showed the only basis of acceptance to God. Even an apostle's *faux pas* was an opportunity to preach the truth.

Paul didn't bring Peter's skeleton out of the closet to make him look bad. The circumcision party had probably told this story to the Galatians, adding a few little twists to "prove" their "gospel." Perhaps it went like this: "We've just been in Antioch and had lunch with Peter. And guess who he wouldn't eat with?...That's right! Gentiles!" Putting a big name behind their lies made it sound convincing.

Well, if that's what they said, they didn't really lie; they just didn't get the whole story out. The truth is, Peter was condemned, not commended, for his actions. Paul then set the record straight for the Galatian believers, offering yet another testimony for the Gospel of grace. Opposed in a hostile environment, the simple Gospel of grace again was highlighted as the only true Gospel.

Peter's motive in all this was the fear of man. His fellowship with Gentiles came to an abrupt halt upon the

Jews' arrival. Fear of man caused him (and others with him) to depart from the simple Gospel. And fear of man continues to pollute the Gospel today.

Newspapers recently ran an article about the bishop of a major denomination who refused to take a definite stand on issues of sexuality. He found himself being pressured by some of his denomination's more "progressive" members to bless "untraditional" unions (including common-law and homosexual marriages). Embracing their stand would cause unpopularity among more conservative members, while denouncing their views would make him equally as unpopular. The answer: remain neutral and please all the people.

This may be an extreme case, but it does illustrate the point. The fear of man takes the Christian farther and farther away from the simple Gospel. Such twentieth-century, man-pleasing churches have a very different basis than the apostolic church of the first century. Jesus gave a simple prerequisite to discipleship: "If any man would come after me, let him deny himself, take up his cross and follow me." Cross-bearing is usually not looked on as a pleasant pastime. In fact, picking up our crosses means that we must empty our hands of a very precious possession: our reputation. Rather than relinquish his good social standing, Peter was ready to sacrifice the true Gospel of grace. Thankfully, Paul could step in and oppose such selfish heresy.

It's important to note, in passing, that heresy is usually self-centered. The simple Gospel of grace is the only "religious" message that strongly teaches the death of self. Most anti-Gospel teachings seek to cater to self. People chant and meditate to find themselves, go through rituals to protect themselves, and basically seek God's blessings for themselves.

Similarly, Peter would have warped the message of grace for the sake of his own reputation. This can happen to the greatest spiritual giant. No one is beyond twisting the Gospel for selfish ambition. Actually, the more well-known the personality, the greater the damage in drawing others away from the Gospel.

Here, Paul confronted Peter's little fling with heresy because Peter's faith, along with pure Christian doctrine, was at stake. Confrontation is an important principle of Christian relationships. Probably the most important teaching on confrontation is found in Matthew 18:15-20. We won't take the time to discuss it here, but if you would like to study the passage, make sure you read the entire chapter. This teaching is sandwiched between a message on "love for all brethren" (18:10-14) and another on "forgiveness" (18:21-22). Confrontation must be seen in light of both.

Paul discerned the actions of Peter and his followers as insincere. Now wasn't Paul becoming just a little judgmental? Hadn't he himself taught that Christians should never judge? Actually, Paul's judgment in this situation was quite appropriate, as Peter wasn't guilty of a private little sin. He made a very loud statement with his nonverbal actions. By refusing to eat with uncircumcised Gentiles, he pronounced them "unclean," that is, not acceptable to God. But God had already shown Peter that Gentiles were no longer to be considered "unclean" (Acts 10). By his actions, he denied the revelation given to him, as well as the entire Gospel of grace.

Paul's argument began with a plea for logic. "If you, though a Jew, live like a Gentile and not like a Jew, how can you compel the Gentiles to live like Jews?" In other words, since Peter didn't depend on circumcision for salvation, how could he ask others to? He was accused of inconsistency.

Many of us know the Gospel and have received the simple message of God's grace through Jesus. But most of us are guilty of the same inconsistency from time to time, when we fail to live accordingly. Our failures are very subtle, often not even recognized as failures. We flatly deny the Gospel when we lay down rules for ourselves and others that will make us more acceptable to God (such as Bible reading, prayer, and right choices). Let's always pray that God would send people to confront us when our lives deny the simple Gospel.

It's always refreshing to see Christians living the Gospel of grace and offering that to others. A British woman named Jackie Pullinger has been ministering to drug addicts in Hong Kong for many years. The people she reaches are very unchurched; some can't even read. Living in terrible bondage to sin, these people could not possibly muster enough effort to save themselves. Yet Jackie offers them their only hope: the grace of God through Jesus. She doesn't give a "quit drugs and then you can come to Jesus" type of message, but simply "come to Jesus, and He will change you." She and those who work with her (including several ex-addicts) are vivid examples of the grace of God lived out.

We note a hint of sarcasm in Paul's next words: "We ourselves, who are Jews by birth and not Gentile sinners..." (v. 15). Jews often referred to Gentiles as sinners, exposing their own sinful pride more than anything else. By using these sarcastic words, he pointed out the same problem in Peter: pride. Really, any tendency toward legalism is based in pride; the successful "do-righter" is placed on a pedestal. From this point on, Paul showed how pride is dealt with from a theological standpoint.

Oh-oh, there's that awful word: *theology*. Time for most Christians' eyelids to become heavy and their minds to close. Actually, the subject isn't as boring as some would make it out to be. In fact, we have been studying theology for the past few chapters, disguising it in terms of experience.

The most important word in the rest of this chapter is

justified. Paul borrowed this word from the Greek court-houses to explain the work Jesus did for man. In ancient Greece, a person would be considered "justified" after being taken to court, tried, and publicly declared "innocent" by the judge. He would be called righteous, an upstanding member of the community.

Paul talked in circles around this word to prove a point: Jesus is our only means of justification. Through the substitution of Christ, God has taken us to court and publicly declared our innocence. He says that we are righteous, and it is *His* perspective on our lives that we must gain. The fourth chapter of Romans paints a beautiful picture of this act of God. He brought us to His court in all our criminal filthiness and accepted the death of Christ as our just punishment. In that same chapter, we see that "Abraham believed in the One who calls the things that are not as if they are." Though we were not righteous, God has the power to call us righteous.

Slander and gossip have grown to horrendous proportions in the Church. Fault-finding is published and marketed, often moving past the confrontation of error into personal bickering. When that is the case, Christians have failed to gain God's view of their righteous brother or sister. You see, we *are* righteous in Christ, *regardless* of how we feel or the mistakes we make. Personal judgments (apart from those which confront sinful actions) have no place in the Church.

Next, Paul phrased the argument most often given against the doctrine of justification by faith: "...if, in our endeavor to be justified in Christ, we ourselves were found to be sinners, is Christ then an agent of sin?" (v. 17). The argument usually runs, "If all we say is 'grace, grace, grace,' how can we live holy lives? We'll be saved, but remain unchanged."

Paul answered this in Romans chapter six with a rhetorical question: "Are we to sin that grace may abound?" This shows the absurdity of such logic. The grace of God should make us want to live ethical lives and make right choices. But our principles must be lived in *response* to God's grace, never to *earn* God's grace. If anyone has the attitude, "Well, I'm saved; I can do what I want now," chances are they haven't really experienced salvation. A regenerated person, indwelt by the Holy Spirit, will begin to share God's hatred of sin. The indwelling Spirit, not our own willpower, is the power that changes us.

In fact, to emphasize human responsibility is sin in itself. "If I build up again those things which I tore down, then I prove myself a transgressor" (v. 18). Paul, the ex-legalist, tore down the Law when he saw Jesus as the means of salvation. To return to a merit system in dealing with God, one rejects God's own method of salvation: the death of Christ. (Romans chapter seven calls this "adultery.") To emphasize any basis of acceptance to God other than Jesus, is sin.

The "build up, tear down" description may be illustrated by thinking of a house. Imagine a very wealthy man gives you several acres of land. On this land stands an old, run-down shack which the wealthy man demolishes. In its place, he builds a beautiful mansion for you to move in to. After a few days in the mansion, you decide you'd rather live in the old shack. You go and find the scraps from its demolition and reconstruct it on your land. By returning to a non-Christ-centered emphasis, the Galatians rebuilt their old shack. And to God, this would be equated with sin.

From here, Paul moved to an unpopular subject: death. "I through the law died to the law, that I might live to God. I have been crucified with Christ..." (19,20). He saw that the true end of the Law is death. Willpower and human goodness could not make God give him eternal life. Crucifixion would be the only answer.

The apostle spoke of such crucifixion several times in the New Testament (Rom. 6; Col. 2,3). The Law had shown him his own dead spiritual state, and he had nailed this dead man to the cross with Christ. Salvation came as he identified with "the One who was made to be sin" for his sake (II Cor. 5:21).

Man must choose between Jesus and the Law. In Romans Paul portrayed the Gospel as a marriage, urging people to choose either Jesus or the Law as their husband. They must come to God by righteousness gained through Christ, or by self-righteousness gained through works. (Remember: one of these is a fragrant aroma to God, the other a wretched stench.)

Paul summarized the first two chapters in verse 21. "I do not nullify the grace of God; for if justification were through the law, then Christ died to no purpose." Herein lies the story of Paul's life. Driven by zeal for the Law, the wickedness of his own heart became painfully obvious when he saw the dazzling beauty of Christ. To move back to a focus other than Jesus would be to return to bondage. If one is justified by what he does, by his own works, the death of Jesus is worthless.

By refusing to eat with uncircumcised Gentiles, Peter denied the significance of Christ's death. His actions told these non-Jews that they needed something more than Jesus to attain fullness of life.

Paul's testimony has shown that Christ alone is the basis of salvation. Jesus, the Author and Finisher of man's faith, was Paul's only hope of righteousness. May our own testimonies declare the same simple Gospel that humbled a religious zealot, overruled the lies of legalists, and corrected a wayward apostle. The Gospel is the only power for salvation.

Questions, Review, and Interpretation

1. What was Paul's revelation? What made this revelation authoritative?

2. Why did Paul refer to his "former manner of life in Judaism"?

3. What is significant about the word *but*, used in verse 15 to show contrast?

4. Why did Paul bring Titus to Jerusalem?

5. Why did Peter refuse to eat with Gentiles? Why did Paul talk about justification in connection with Peter's table manners?

Application:

1. Make up one sentence that describes your pre-Christian life, and then write "but God..." to show that He stepped in to save you.

2. God had set a time to reveal His Son to Paul. From your own testimony, think of three or four ways that God ordered your circumstances or thoughts to prepare you for your revelation.

3. What are some marks of false brethren (like the circumcision party) or true believers (like Titus) in our twentieth-century church?

4. What are some ways that we can "fight" for the Gospel of grace?

5. What external standards are wrongly placed on Christians before they are made to feel welcome in our fellowships?

Part Four

The History of Grace:
Before the Baby-sitter

7

Bewitched by the Law

O foolish Galatians! Who has bewitched you, before whose eyes Jesus Christ was publicly portrayed as crucified? Let me ask you only this: Did you receive the Spirit by works of the law, or by hearing with faith? Are you so foolish? Having begun with the Spirit, are you now ending with the flesh? Did you experience so many things in vain?—if it really is in vain. Does he who supplies the Spirit to you and works miracles among you do so by works of the law, or by hearing with faith?

Galatians 3:1-5

In spite of pleasant old TV shows, witches are seldom seen as respectable middle-class people married to mortals. Most Christians are shocked (or at least repulsed) by the thought of witchcraft. How much more shocking to actually be described as "bewitched." Such is the fate of legalistic Christianity.

It was now time for the Galatians to become offended and to apply Paul's first two chapters. He had made some plain statements about what constitutes salvation. These may be condensed to three words: faith in Jesus. He had also gone to great lengths to show what doesn't save a person: anything other than Jesus. Through a series of rhetorical questions, Paul then brought his message down to their own level. It was vital that these straying Galatians see the foolishness of departing from the simple Gospel of grace.

Rhetorical questions are usually tinged with cynicism. A nagging wife will ask her lazy husband, glued to the TV, "Are you too busy to take out the garbage?" She doesn't expect an answer. Rather, through a sarcastic tone, she points out her husband's unacceptable actions.

Paul was about to discuss Abraham, the father of all Jews. The old saying, "Like father, like son," is not without truth. A son is usually marked with his father's characteristics, including physical and emotional features. Jews felt that sharing Abraham's circumcision ritual marked them as his true sons. Paul showed that true sons of Abraham bear a far more important trait of that man of God.

Of the five opening questions in this chapter, three were really a plea for common sense. In fact, Paul began by calling the Galatians "foolish." He repeated this term in verse three. In the Phillips translation, they are called "idiots" (v. 1) and "stupid" (v. 3).

Was Paul merely venting his frustration by stooping to name-calling? About then, most of us "Christian-unity referees" would have penalized him for a lack of tact. But Paul's assessments were accurate, because departing from the very foundation stone of faith is the most disastrous thing a Christian can do. This series of questions will help us to understand why.

Question #1: "Who has bewitched you, before whose eyes Jesus was publicly portrayed as crucified?" (v. 1).

Paul asked a "who" question, although fully aware of the guilty party's identity. He realized that members of the circumcision party, preaching a distorted Gospel, were the culprits. Paul didn't expect an answer to his "who" question; he had answered it himself in the first two chapters. Rather, his emphasis was placed upon the word *bewitched*. The Greek root word refers to casting a spell or placing a hex on someone. By turning away from the simple Gospel to the Law, the Galatians actually became involved in something that resembled witchcraft. This is God's understanding of legalism.

Why is witchcraft viewed as wrong? Because someone other than God is being given control of a life. Pastors barely even need to mention that seances and Ouija boards are off limits. But legalism, carrying such "fine, upstanding young man" looks, seems far more acceptable. We know the Bible denounced it, but few escape its trap. The "I've been good, so now God will bless me" mentality is man-centered legalism. And as far as God is concerned, this equals witchcraft. There is a basic similarity between one controlled by evil spirits and one controlled by his own willpower: both are godless.

Farther along Paul made a statement about "turning back again to the weak and beggarly elemental spirits" (4:9). He was referring to certain kinds of Gentile traditions, mystery religions involving the worship of demons. In another passage, he mentioned that during his days as "church exterminator," he was also enslaved to "the elemental spirits" (4:3). The grace of Jesus had delivered them from this slavery. Why return to it?

The crucified Jesus had spared the Galatians from eternal bondage to mystery religions and elemental spirits. The same crucified Jesus would spare them from another type of slavery: legalistic Christianity.

Question #2: "Did you receive the Spirit by the works of the Law or by hearing with faith?"

Most of the Galatians would have their hands up, ready to give the correct answer to this one. Of course, works of the Law had nothing to do with their salvation. In fact, as pagans involved with mystery religions, they would have had no interest in the Law of Moses, and most had probably never even heard of it. So the Law played no part in their salvation. Two other words reveal how they had obtained salvation: hearing and faith. We could also use the words, "hearing and believing." The Galatians had *heard* the Gospel, *believed* the Gospel (that is, they accepted the death of Jesus for their individual lives), and that was that. They were saved.

The only problem with this formula is its simplicity. In fact, it seems too simple for most intelligent human beings to base their lives on. But, as Paul showed in this paragraph, deviating from the simple Gospel is actually the height of ignorance.

Think back to your own salvation experience. Were any works outlined as a means of coming to God? Did one who witnessed to you say, "Read the Bible, pray, don't smoke, don't drink; Okay...now you're saved." It's doubtful that these were laid down for you as "rules of salvation." If they were, you probably joined a cult.

How ironic that Christians place duties on themselves after their salvation experience. Again, please don't misread our words. We firmly believe that Bible reading, prayer, and right living are appropriate marks of a Christian. But none of these can possibly commend one to God.

The death of Jesus, the substitute for our own deserved punishment, is our only means of commendation to God. In God's eyes, every form of righteousness—except righteousness through faith in Christ—bears a remarkable resemblance to dung (Phil. 3:8,9).

Question #3: "Having begun with the Spirit, are you now ending with the flesh?"

By beginning with the Spirit, the Galatians had accepted the righteousness supernaturally bestowed upon them by God. By "ending with the flesh," they sought additional righteousness through self-effort. They could be compared to a hitchhiker, promised a ride all the way to his destination. Halfway there, he yells, "Stop the car, I'll walk from here." Weariness and blisters are preferred to the driver's gracious offer.

Instead of looking to Jesus as the means of their salvation, the Galatians looked to programs for spiritual betterment. Maybe their weekly schedule began something like this:

Monday—Overview of the Law

Tuesday—Beginning Circumcision and
        True Spirituality

Wednesday—Advanced Circumcision or
          Surgical Techniques

Again, let us clarify that we are not opposed to schedules or programs. We are merely coming against the thought of sanctification through anything other than the Person and Work of Jesus Christ.

The legalistic Christian may be compared to an overweight lady who decides to go on a diet. After a few months, and twenty lost pounds, the goal of slenderness is within reach but not yet attained. The lady grows tired of her diet and decides she can look slimmer by simply wearing different styles of clothing. She may appear slim, but the truth hasn't changed. She's still overweight and worries constantly about how she looks to others.

This analogy contains more truth than meets the eye. The legalistic Christian may have an appearance of godliness, but the very means of godliness is missing: the grace of God. And besides, all his Christian works, uninspired by the Spirit, will prove to be both uncomfortable and unnatural.

Question #4: "Did you experience so many things in vain?—if it really is in vain."

The Christian life should be rich with experiences through God. The Galatians had not exactly missed out on "good times" in the Lord. Paul may have been helping them remember some of the following:

• The miracles they had observed

- The salvation they had experienced

- The persecution they had suffered

The importance of such experiences decreases when a Christian adopts a legalistic lifestyle. Legalism usually results in conformity to the world rather than transformation of the person. (In other words, legalism helps us to "not be too fanatical.") The challenge is simple: don't throw away your invaluable inheritance in Christ by gathering the worthless trash of self-righteousness.

Moving past a grace-oriented life is a very real problem facing Christians, both at personal and corporate levels. Many Christian organizations have begun with a dynamic, vibrant spirit, marked by Christ-centered living. Over the years, some of these have failed to keep the Cross of Christ central, and have basically become secular organizations. The Christian experience becomes mediocre when the simple Gospel is neglected.

Question #5: "Does he who supplies the Spirit to you and works miracles among you do so by works of the law, or by hearing with faith?"

There are those two words again: *hearing* and *faith* (or believing). The Galatians had experienced so much with those two simple words that they couldn't afford to live otherwise. By referring to their faith in Christ, Paul reminded them of the supernatural. God works miracles because He is gracious, not because His people press the right buttons.

Hearing is a passive act (that is, it can't be helped), and therefore does not commend one to God. Believing is an attitude which God enables us to have, for Jesus is the Author of our faith. Hearing and believing are childlike concepts. Anyone can do them. Childlikeness should mark our entire Christian experience, even as we grow to maturity. In fact, true maturity is mastering this basic, childlike faith in God. Christians must never move beyond "hearing and believing."

A missionary friend once transported four ladies through the Moroccan desert in his Volkswagen. The car broke down hours from civilization, and the five sat stranded in the hot desert sun. With food and water scarce, motorists uncommon on this road, and roving bands of rapists a very real threat, they became understandably concerned for their safety.

Wondering which way to begin walking for help, our friend asked God for direction. He heard the Lord say, "Stay put," and although that seemed a bit ridiculous, the group remained in the Volkswagen. They sat and waited for any sign of help. After two days, a vehicle pulled up behind them. The driver just happened to be a Volkswagen repairman with the part needed to fix the broken-down car. The car was repaired, and the five stranded people drove on their way, none the worse for wear.

Hearing and believing really does work. It's the simple method through which God saved us. And it is the means by which we live the Christian life. Back to the "witchcraft" example, the Christian who doesn't live by "hearing and faith" may do some acceptable Christian things, but he's not empowered by God. In reality, he's under the spell of his own weak Law-keeping will.

8

The Curse that Blesses Many

Thus Abraham "believed God, and it was reckoned to him as righteousness." So you see that it is men of faith who are the sons of Abraham. And the scripture, foreseeing that God would justify the Gentiles by faith, preached the gospel beforehand to Abraham, saying, "In you shall all the nations be blessed." So then, those who are men of faith are blessed with Abraham who had faith.

For all who rely on works of the law are under a curse; for it is written, "Cursed be every one who does not abide by all things written in the book of the law, and do them." Now it is evident that no man is justified before God by the law; for "He who through faith is righteous shall live"; but the law does not rest on faith, for "He who does them shall live by them." Christ redeemed us from the curse of the law, having become a curse for us—for it is written, "Cursed be every one who hangs on a tree"—that in Christ Jesus the blessing of Abraham might come upon the Gentiles, that we might receive the promise of the Spirit through faith.

Galatians 3:6-14

What does a blessing have in common with a curse? Although the word is usually only heard in church, the concept of "blessing" is packed with meaning. Of course, we know that "curse" is opposite to "blessing," so the words really have nothing in common. Or do they?

Chapters three and four of Galatians teach about the history of grace, taking us all the way back to Abraham. The blessing of which Paul spoke began with this great man who lived nearly 2,000 years before Christ. People have always had the opportunity to share this blessing, and we have that same opportunity today.

Paul began with a quote that summed up the life of this patriarch: he "believed God, and it was reckoned to him as righteousness" (v. 6). Faith in God marked Abraham's life, and, in God's eyes, that made him righteous. Paul took this quotation from Genesis 15:6, so it is important that we study that passage to learn what made Abraham's faith so special. Abraham gave us a very honest picture of what it means to walk with God. We'll never be asked to sacrifice our children or to father an entire nation. Still, Abraham's faith is held up as an ideal, something that should mark each child of God.

The first obvious trait of faith-filled Abraham is his realism. In Genesis 15, God told Abraham not to worry because he would receive a great reward. We would expect such a man of faith to respond with a great statement of faith. Something like, "Amen. I believe it. The reward is mine!" Well, if that's what we're looking for, Abraham's answer will be somewhat disappointing. Rather than mouthing some positive confession that he didn't really believe, Abraham spoke his heart, and flatly questioned God's promise!

God had promised to make Abraham (actually at this point his name was still Abram) into a great nation. Having no children and being well past the age of childbearing, Abraham found the promise unbelievable. He needed much more than a positive confession on which to base his faith. He basically told God that his hopes of receiving such a reward were swiftly fading. The great man of faith failed to "confess and possess," or to "name and claim."

Today, some Christians base their faith on the words they speak. Those who are sick are taught to say, "I'm not sick"; those unemployed, living in the slums, are taught to confess, "I have much money"; and those on their deathbeds are taught to deny the prospect of death. These confessions deny reality. Such attempts at faith fall far short of the faith of Abraham and are often based in pride.

In his challenging book *Humility*, Andrew Murray presents a definition of faith when he asks, "Is it not the confession of nothingness and helplessness, the surrender and waiting to let God work? Is it not in itself the most humbling thing there can be—the acceptance of our place as dependents, who can claim or get or do nothing but what grace bestows?"

Abraham showed the same realism before God in Genesis 17. Here God changed Abram's name to Abraham, which means "father of a multitude." If the promise seemed far-fetched the first time, now it appeared utterly ridiculous! By now, Abraham was 99 years old, and his wife Sarah was 89. Any hopes for a child were, naturally speaking, lost. Abraham's response? He fell on his face laughing. His attitude was basically one of, "Come on, God, let's get serious." Hmm...such negative confessions are not going to inherit promises, are they? It's true that the man who doubts will not receive anything from the Lord, and Abraham did have his doubts straightened out eventually. But these doubts were not quelled through his own words. They melted as he listened to God and believed on Him.

Why are we going to such great lengths to highlight Abraham's doubts when we are supposed to be discussing his faith? Actually, we are trying to highlight the object of Abraham's faith. He didn't grunt and grimace, trying to work up enough resolve to believe the promise. Rather, as Paul said, he "believed God."

This is the simple faith that made Abraham righteous. He eventually resigned himself to the fact that God had made an impossible promise, and God would have to turn it into a reality. This is Gospel faith. God has proclaimed justification through faith to all who believe. One look at our filthy, sinful hearts should make that proclamation appear as ridiculous to us as the promise appeared to Abraham. But as with Abraham, we also deem God able to do that which He promises. Impossible as it should seem in the natural, God can make us, the foulest of sinners, clean.

"So...it is men of faith who are the sons of Abraham" (v. 7). Unfortunately for the circumcision party, nice little external qualities do not entitle one to sonship. All their works made them counterfeit children.

Imagine a fisherman with his sons. Living at home, these children hear and learn "fishing talk," about how their father uses certain types of nets and lines, and about how he lost the "big one." But they will not know how to fish for themselves unless they actually go out in the boat with their father and do what he does. In the same way, Abraham's true sons share his life of faith, not merely his external markings of circumcision.

The "Abraham Plan," our term for the historic Gospel, had been in effect for centuries before Jesus. Through Abraham, God had already decided to bless all nations, not just a few Jews. People are blessed as they believe God in the way Abraham believed Him. We'll consider the Abraham Plan more as we study further in chapters three and four of Galatians. For now, we will say that it has been God's eternal plan to justify all by faith alone.

In summary, it is through faith in God that we share Abraham's blessing of righteousness. As Abraham's faith in God enabled him to be called righteous, so our faith in

God does the same. In verses 10-14, Paul's attention turns from the "blessing" to the "curse."

Now that we know who is blessed, let's take a look at who receives the curse. "All who rely on works of the law are under a curse..." (v. 10). A curse awaits anyone who fails to live up to all aspects of the Law. This eliminates the Jewish mentality (and that of many Christians) of the great heavenly scale which weighs good works against bad, and deals out rewards accordingly.

Basically, Paul was saying that a sinner cannot plead his case with "I've only sinned a little." A murderer does not have charges dropped against him because he didn't steal. A drunk driver is no less guilty because he didn't commit arson. A sinner is no less sinful because he did some nice things in his life. James summed it up well with "Whoever keeps the whole law but fails in one point has become guilty of all of it" (James 2:10). The question is not, "Which law have you broken?" but "Whose Law have you broken?"

God has laid down a standard of perfection which no man can possibly keep. Does that make Him an ogre? No. He realizes that all fall short of His perfect legal standards. God does not expect anyone to keep the entire Law, but He has given a way to escape the curse. The way to escape the curse is mentioned in Galatians 3:13. We will save an extended discussion of this until later.

In verse 10, Paul quoted from Deuteronomy 27:26, the last of a long list of curses. Moses had claimed that a curse awaited anyone who did not live by the Law. Since no one has kept every "jot and tittle," all can expect to receive that curse. God's perfect standard, the Law, shows that all Law-breakers have offended His holiness, and must receive the death penalty.

So, whereas Abraham had depended on God for righteousness, his Jewish descendants decided to trust in their own Law-keeping abilities. Similarly the circumcision party attempted to alter the simple-faith focus of the Galatian Christians. Rather than trusting in God alone for their righteousness, these young Christians were being asked to trust their own works to make them righteous.

Many Christians believe that the words, "God helps those who help themselves," are found in the Bible. Actually, Benjamin Franklin, not God, coined this saying. It contains some truth, but it is not a scriptural basis for one's walk with God. A more biblical concept would be phrased, "God helps those who are helpless." Jesus said, "Blessed are the poor in spirit, for theirs is the kingdom of heaven" (Matt. 5:3). It is those who see themselves as spiritually impoverished who can enter God's kingdom.

Have you ever felt more worthy to be in God's presence on some days than at other times? Maybe you've read your Bible regularly or possibly been out feeding the hungry. Because of these good works, it seems especially easy to converse with God, and even easier to expect blessings from Him. Remember the Pharisee and the publican (Luke 18:9-14). One came to God, feeling quite deserving of His presence. The other came with shame, knowing that only God's grace would allow him to be heard. With whom was God pleased?

"He who through faith is righteous shall live" (v. 11). This quotation from Habakkuk 2:4 is found three times in the New Testament (see also Romans 1:17; Hebrews 10:38). The motto of the Reformation, this one little Scripture was used by God to totally realign the spiritual atmosphere of Europe under Martin Luther. Paul placed this verse in his letter to give a stark contrast between "Gospel-followers" and "Law-lovers." The Gospel is something which God does for man; the Law is something which man does for God.

We can think of this concept in terms of a prisoner and a king. Hoping for a pardon, the prisoner sits in his cell, continually making gifts for the king. With these, he hopes to sway the king's favor in his direction. The only problem is that these gifts remain in the cell, and are never seen by the king, who lives far away. One day, for no apparent reason, the king unlocks the prison door, pardoning the prisoner and setting him free. The gifts played no part in his decision.

In the same way, God does not pardon us because of our "gifts" of right living to Him. Far removed because of our sin, we are pardoned by God simply because He is kind and merciful. Our acts of righteousness, if they are intended to earn our salvation, mean nothing to Him. We base our faith on the fact that God has done things for us, not on our desires to do things for God.

The death of Jesus is God's ultimate work for man. When the Cross ceases to be central to our churches and to our individual lives, we quickly fall into the trap of performing for God. "Christ redeemed us from the curse of the law, having become a curse for us..." (v. 13). Jesus took our curse upon Himself. The substitutionary death of Jesus is a theme central to the New Testament. Here we see that He became a curse for us. The Corinthians learned that Jesus actually became sin for them (II Cor. 5:21). The Romans were told that Jesus bore God's wrath for them (Rom. 3). The Cross is the greatest picture in the world of God's love, for it is the place where God "laid down His life for his friends" (John 15:13).

God's perfect standards of justice demand that He punish sin. Imagine a judge who waffles on his judgments when trying lawbreakers. He might say, "Oh, that's okay, just try not to murder anymore." He may be merciful, but certainly not just. God's attribute of justice causes Him to punish sin, even when found in His own Son. Jesus averted God's wrath from us to Himself.

That brings us back to the blessing. "...That in Christ Jesus the blessing of Abraham might come upon the Gentiles, that we might receive the promise of the Spirit through faith" (v. 14). In our study, we have traveled in a full circle, and have returned to the blessing. We're ready to answer the question posed at the beginning of this chapter, "What does a blessing have in common with a curse?" You have realized by now that both are met in Jesus. He who carried the curse of the Law for us enables us to share in the blessing of Abraham. Jesus is both our "curse-bearer" and our "blessing-bestower."

Through Him, the promise of the Spirit is more than just a promise to believers. Jews in the Old Testament were made aware of the Spirit from time to time. There were stories of exceptional people whom the Spirit would occasionally visit and empower for special tasks. Through Jesus, the occasional visitor has become a permanent guest. God lives inside us!

The Spirit is the resident who lives in our hearts through faith. He does not live there because we have swept the house and made it tidy for Him. He comes and arranges the house the way He deems best. That means He is the house guest who has taken over and is in control of household activities. (We often grow tired of house guests who dominate our space. In the same way, it may seem uncomfortable for the Holy Spirit to guide our lives in the way He desires.) This is the difference between working *for* God, and working *with* God. With the indwelling Spirit, our works are done as a response to God's goodness, by God's power.

Jesus described the Holy Spirit as One who would flow like rivers of living waters from our hearts (John 7:36-39). Trying to earn God's grace with our own strength and willpower is like offering Him trickles of polluted water, filled with the trash of our wicked hearts. Through the Holy Spirit, the water is cleansed, the pollution eliminated, the trash removed, and the trickle becomes a river of living water. Which would you prefer?

9

Before the Baby-sitter

To give a human example, brethren: no one annuls even a man's will, or adds to it, once it has been ratified. Now the promises were made to Abraham and to his offspring. It does not say, "And to offsprings," referring to many; but, referring to one, "And to your offspring," which is Christ. This is what I mean: the law, which came four hundred and thirty years afterward, does not annul a covenant previously ratified by God, so as to make the promise void. For if the inheritance is by the law, it is no longer by promise; but God gave it to Abraham by a promise.

Why then the law? It was added because of transgressions, till the offspring should come to whom the promise had been made; and it was ordained by angels through an intermediary. Now an intermediary implies more than one; but God is one.

Is the law then against the promises of God? Certainly not; for if a law had been given which could make alive, then righteousness would indeed be by the law. But the scripture consigned all things to sin, that what was promised to faith in Jesus Christ might be given to those who believe.

Galatians 3:15-22

A favorite story line is that of a wealthy old man planning to bestow his vast riches on some fortunate heir. In such stories, a number of characters make attempts at persuading the old man to leave his money to them. During his final days, everyone tries to treat him nicely. The fortune-seekers bring gifts, visit, and do everything possible trying to tip his scales of money in their favor.

By using the Law as their basis of acceptance, the Jews treated God in much the same way. They had an attitude of, "Be nice to the Old Guy, and He'll be nice to us." And therein, the circumcision party failed to remember their own Jewish history, much less the sovereign nature of God.

God's will had been ratified centuries before by His own word. (Most human wills are ratified by signatures.) He had given a promise to Abraham; the promise of an inheritance. As Paul said, not even a human will can be changed once it is ratified. Certainly, God's plan of inheritance is not subject to change.

As explained in the preceding chapter, the Abraham Plan was set in motion many years before Christ. Three aspects of this plan should be briefly mentioned. Firstly, *God planned to bless all nations through Abraham* (Gen. 12:1-3; Gal. 3:8). God had much further-reaching goals than to shower just a few circumcised Jews with His blessings.

Secondly, the Abraham Plan *has been fulfilled in Christ*. "Now the promises were made to Abraham and to his offspring...which is Christ" (v. 16). The word *offspring* is to be understood as a single person. Paul took the Spirit-inspired liberty of interpreting this offspring as Jesus. At times, it may seem a bit difficult to understand Paul's rhetoric, but the point he made was quite simple: *Jesus is the means by which God blesses the world!* He is the special component in the plot of history, brought in by God, the Master Strategist.

The third aspect of the Abraham Plan is that it remains unaffected by the Law. "The law, which came four hundred and thirty years afterward, does not annul a covenant previously ratified by God, so as to make the promise void" (v. 17). In other words, the introduction of the Law did not add to or take away from the Abraham Plan. The inheritance was, is, and will be given by God's gracious promise.

With all that said, it's about time to measure the circumcision party by this Abraham Plan as they tried to earn their inheritance with some nice works. Ironically, their works were preventing them from gaining God's blessing. Their hands were meant to be empty, held up to God in helpless surrender, ready to receive His grace. Instead they became filled with self-righteous offerings of trash. As already pointed out, Abraham had absolutely no way of making God's promise work. The Abraham Plan depends totally upon God's grace. The circumcision party, on the other hand, depended on self-effort.

Do we receive God's blessings as *unworthy* Christians? Or do we expect God's blessings because we've been *good* Christians? When you've had a bad day (the car breaks down, you burn dinner, unexpected expenses dry up your wallet), do you feel like God is punishing you for not reading your Bible, or for not making a right choice? If so, you'd probably feel quite comfortable with the circumcision party.

All this talk about "inheritance" gives us an interesting picture of God. He is the wealthy owner of everything good. The greatest possession that He bestows on His children is righteousness. The only stipulation for the heirs is that they believe He can give that which He promised. Through simple faith in Jesus, God has given a rich inheritance to all who believe Him.

"Why then the law?" (v. 19). Paul anticipated the question which was certainly foremost in the minds of his dear Galatians. If God's plan had always been to dole out righteousness as a favor, why did He even bother to lay down the Law? Who needs rules, anyway? The Galatians were about to learn the real purpose of the Law of Moses.

"It was added because of transgressions..." (v. 19). A transgression occurs when one oversteps his bounds. In other words, God has drawn boundaries and placed "No Trespassing" signs around them. Though we see the signs, we deliberately ignore them and step over the line anyway. Adam and Eve's fruit dinner may be termed a transgression.

So firstly, the Law existed to help people see life's "No Trespassing" signs. As people sometimes fail to keep off the grass when asked to, so the Jews managed to overstep the bounds of God's laws. The Law points out the actual events of sin. J.B. Phillips translated this concept descriptively by saying that God gave us the Law as "a straightedge to show us how crooked we are."

Scripture details other purposes of the Law. A second purpose similar to the first is that the Law reveals the sinful condition of our hearts (Rom. 7:13). James described the Law as a mirror (James 1:23,24). Through this passage in Romans, Paul described which type of mirror it may be compared to; the Law functions like a convex mirror, the kind at a circus. As a convex mirror makes objects appear bigger than they actually are, so the pure Law reflects clearly a heart's sinful desires.

In other words, if a man is a thief, when he reads the Ten Commandments, the one about stealing is going to be the passage that literally dominates his view of the rest. Just like one of those mirrors at the circus.

For example, many people struggle with lust. The Law clearly prohibits sexual sins such as adultery, fornication, and other types. The one who lusts will see these rules and realize that his desires are wrong. Of course, mere statements don't give the least bit of help to overcome lust. The strength to not sin must come from elsewhere. But the point is, as the Law clearly condemns sexual sin, the one who lusts will clearly see the sin of his own heart.

Thirdly, the Law serves as a valuable teaching tool (II Tim. 3:16). Certain principles in the Law reveal God's attitude about life. He hates killing, stealing, and adultery; He cares for the poor and oppressed, and wants His people to do the same. Sharing these attitudes, or keeping most of the rules, does not provide a ticket to eternal life. Nowhere does the Bible teach that Law-keepers on earth will be doorkeepers in heaven. Only the righteousness of Christ makes us acceptable to God.

Notice the next word in Galatians 3:19: *until*. We've studied a few purposes for the Law. This little word shows the temporary quality of the Law. It was given "until the offspring should come to whom the promise had been made." The Law served a specific purpose in Old Testament times. It serves fewer purposes in New Testament days. And throughout all history, it contains no power to save. Here again, Paul pointed to the superiority of the promise—the blessing to all nations—of righteousness through faith.

So far, we've seen that the Law is inferior to the Gospel in both purpose and durability. The Law condemns and fades. The Gospel makes righteous and stands forever. Now we'll observe another way in which the Law pales beside the simple Gospel.

"...It was ordained by angels through an intermediary. Now an intermediary implies more than one; but God is one" (vv. 19,20). Common Jewish belief held that angels received the Law from God and delivered it to Moses, who in turn related it to the people. Such a nice supernatural story would elevate this rule book to enormous heights of respect!

The "but God is one" phrase shows that the Gospel's

introduction into the world is superior to that of the Law. Whereas mere angels delivered the written code, God Himself delivers the Gospel. God stepped into history in the Person of Jesus and lived the Gospel for man. Paul personally received the Gospel through a firsthand encounter with God. In the same way, the Galatians had met God personally when they received the message.

What an amazing concept! The God of the universe has come to us personally. The Gospel message is obviously very important to Him, too important to send by a mere delivery boy or angel. The Galatians were being asked to sacrifice this Gospel and to give up direct relationship with God. The circumcision party wanted them to have a relationship with a rule book given by angels instead.

Sometimes Christians do the same when they become so "Bible-based" that their lives are lived by principle rather than by God's Spirit. God Himself has introduced the Gospel to us that we might not only be saved through it, but also live by it. Many Christians have begun with zeal but faded with rules. They have "learned how to live the Christian life," and therefore don't really need God.

Since the Gospel is so superior, "is the law then against the promises of God?" (v. 21). Although they serve separate purposes, the Law is not opposed to God's promises. It would be some mismatch if the two actually vied with each other to be the basis for blessing, like a professional boxer being challenged by his wimpy water boy. The water boy does serve a role, but he isn't meant to take on championship fighters!

God never intended to make people alive by the Law. Rather, "the scripture consigned all things to sin, that what was promised to faith in Christ Jesus might be given to those who believe" (v. 22). In II Corinthians 3:7-9, the Law is called a "dispensation of condemnation" and a "dispensation of death." In the Greek language, the "all things" of verse 23 is neither masculine nor feminine. It is a neuter word that covers everything, including man and all that he does. In other words, man's life apart from God is best characterized by one word: sin.

Through Christ alone, believers have gained righteousness, the promise given to Abraham. We repeat, through Christ alone—not through confessions, willpower, or ministry techniques—do we know deliverance from sin.

By embracing the Law, the Galatians clung to something outdated and useless. Such foolishness would be worse than a major airline deciding to replace their passenger jetliners with twin-seater, open-cockpit propeller planes. As old-fashioned airplanes are unreliable and prone to crashes, so the life of a legalistic Christian is destined to burst into flames.

The Law does not give life. Do we live the Christian life by principle and precept, or by the power of the Spirit? Do we teach others the rules of Christianity, or do we point them to the life-changing God? Fruit-bearing marks the true disciple of Christ. We must make disciples who are dead to the Law (self-righteousness), but alive to Christ.

Smith Wigglesworth, a dynamic evangelist in the early 1900s, understood this idea. With a ministry that breathed the supernatural, he found this concept the major key to living a supernatural Christian life. He would often say that as a person is totally dead to the Law, the Spirit's life-giving power can freely flow through him.

Should we throw out ethics and morals? No. We are to be people of principles. But God is far greater than our principles. We approach Him always with empty hands, asking for more grace to live for Him.

The Galatians had to wait until the end of this letter to learn the correct place of ethics. As typical people, they were eager to place the cart before the horse, stressing human responsibility above God's gracious working. But the message was clear: a good life is useless if the goodness issues from a wicked heart.

10

Firing the Baby-sitter

Now before faith came, we were confined under the law, kept under restraint until faith should be revealed. So that the law was our custodian until Christ came, that we might be justified by faith. But now that faith has come, we are no longer under a custodian; for in Christ Jesus you are all sons of God, through faith. For as many of you as were baptized into Christ have put on Christ. There is neither Jew nor Greek, there is neither slave nor free, there is neither male nor female; for you are all one in Christ Jesus. And if you are Christ's, then you are Abraham's offspring, heirs according to promise.

I mean that the heir, as long as he is a child, is no better than a slave, though he is the owner of all the estate; but he is under guardians and trustees until the date set by the father. So with us; when we were children, we were slaves to the elemental spirits of the universe. But when the time had fully come, God sent forth his Son, born of woman, born under the law, to redeem those who were under the law, so that we might receive adoption as sons. And because you are sons, God has sent the Spirit of his Son into our hearts, crying, "Abba! Father!" So through God you are no longer a slave but a son, and if a son then an heir. Galatians 3:23 to 4:7

In this passage, Paul gives many different illustrations of how the legalistic Christian may appear. Each one sheds light on a different facet and can help us see the total picture.

It's interesting to watch parents trying to sneak out on their children. Often the child will realize something is wrong as soon as the baby-sitter arrives. Then the unfortunate sitter is often left with an evening of trying to stifle the screams of the deserted child.

In these verses, Paul made an analogy portraying the Law as a baby-sitter. Greek parents often hired a custodian (v. 24) to watch over the children for long periods of time. This custodian—or baby-sitter, as we will call him—would take care of the child from about age six until maturity. In a sense, the child would have little freedom under his baby-sitter, and, in many respects, the Law is like this. We'll look more at this analogy in a little while. For now, remember that throughout this book, Paul contrasted the binding Law with freeing faith. The baby-sitter analogy continues this contrast.

"Before faith came, we were confined under the law, kept under restraint until faith should be revealed" (v. 23). The word *faith* in this situation is used as a *metonymy*. That means it takes the place of another noun. Verses 24 and 25 also speak of something that "came": in verse 24, Christ came; while in verse 25, Paul stated again that faith came. So, the words *faith* and *Christ* are inseparably bound together. God-pleasing faith has no object other than Jesus.

For a simple example, let's take another look at the chair illustration. No one eyes a three-legged chair with broken springs and shaky frame and says, "I'm such a good chair-sitter; this chair will certainly hold me up." As faith in one's chair-sitting ability is unable to keep one secure in a broken chair, so faith in one's Law-keeping ability is unable to keep one secure with God. Only a good chair supplies faith to sit, and Christ alone supplies faith to live.

Paul painted pre-Christ days of history as a picture of confinement. The Law acted as a type of prison cell, imprisoning all until the "Key" to freedom would come. The Galatians were now being asked to give up such freedom and return to their old prison cells.

Now that Paul's audience understood the bondage concept, he began to talk about the custodian, or baby-sitter. "The law was our custodian until Christ came" (v. 24). As already explained, Greek parents hired custodians to watch over and train their children. Greek classical literature contains references to them. People often talked about their custodians with great bitterness, although later in life, some appreciated the disciplines learned. Few looked on their baby-sitters with love.

Paul painted exactly the same picture of the Law. It did serve a purpose in teaching principles and disciplines, but as the baby-sitter is a temporary helper until the parent comes, so the Law is an inferior teacher to Christ. The Law kept people in bondage until Christ would justify them by faith. "But now that faith has come, we are no longer under a custodian; for in Christ Jesus you are all sons of God, through faith" (vv. 25,26). Now that Jesus has come, it is time to fire the baby-sitter! The Law kept people waiting for Jesus. Through its high ideals, man is pointed to a greater enabling Power.

Certainly Greek children longed for the day when their baby-sitters would look for another job. For them, this happened at the "age of maturity." Jesus is the mark of Christian maturity.

If we continue with this analogy, we can say that legalism is a form of childishness. (Not to be confused with childlikeness—a good quality for Christians, referring to humility and innocence.) Often, we call someone a "mature" Christian if he does all the correct "Christian things," and lives by all the right "Christian rules." The truly mature Christian, on the other hand, has learned to live by the Spirit. Right living is merely an outflow of his walk with Jesus.

The Spirit, not a rule book, must govern one's Christian experience. (Actually, we usually give the rules a much more spiritual name, *principles*.) Neither is a Christian's experience governed by a pastor, leader, or Christian brother.

Sometimes missionaries remain on the mission field long after that particular call of God on their lives has been fulfilled. Why? Because missions are very important to God and all concerned, so it must be the "spiritual thing to do." Those missionaries' lives are based on an unwritten rule book rather than a daily walk with God.

The life of Jesus, not rules, must mark the believer. "For as many of you as were baptized into Christ have put on Christ" (v. 27). Jesus is the garment worn by Christians, the robe of righteousness covering all who ask for it. The circumcision party deemed such a garment as insufficient covering. To them the evidence of a true believer should be the mark of circumcision.

Jews were quite proud of this little mark that set them apart as God's covenant people. Are we proud of our little Christian works that make us appear "holier-than-all-other-thou's?" May God always remind us of the shameful nakedness that only the robe of righteousness, given through Jesus, can cover. All external barriers between people are broken down through Jesus. "There is neither Jew nor Greek, there is neither slave nor free, there is neither male nor female; for you are all one in Christ Jesus" (v. 28). All racial, social, and sexual barriers are demolished through His work on the Cross. Jesus alone is the identifying mark of all His people.

In many respects, the circumcision party based their teaching on the concept of Jewish superiority. Jews placed

Gentiles in the same category as dogs and pigs. Greeks, the originators of Western thought and culture, considered themselves so far above everyone else that no one else could even seriously be considered. But in Jesus, neither Jew nor Greek may claim superiority. All *racial* barriers are demolished through Christ.

The same could be said of slaves and free men. Although slaves were usually treated somewhat decently in Roman culture, they were still viewed as second-class people. Paul never attempted to abolish an unjust social structure; rather he pointed out the truth that in Christ, both slaves and free are equal. They both wear the same uniform, the robe of righteousness. All *social* barriers are destroyed through Christ.

The final category, men and women, teaches the same truth. The women's liberation movement had not been founded in Paul's day, and certainly Paul would not be behind many of its ideals. But ancients viewed slaves and women as substandard, weak and inferior. More than any other group, true Christians have elevated the position of women in society. Role distinctions are not removed, but women are given the same importance as men. In Christ, all *sexual* barriers are removed.

All are one in Christ. Every person who names the name of Jesus, trusting Him for salvation, is part of that oneness. Regardless of race, sex, position, or depth of sin committed, we are all one in Christ. This oneness is especially significant in light of the word *offspring.* "And if you are Christ's, then you are Abraham's offspring, heirs according to promise" (v. 29). The offspring here is also singular, only now it refers to an entire group of people. The point is that we as believers are so identified with Jesus the offspring, that we, too, are called "offspring" of Abraham.

The point of this theology is simple: the identification mark of a Christian is Jesus. Actions, attitudes, and words must reflect the Jesus who lives inside every believer.

In considering the greatness of Jesus, do you see what a minor thing the Galatians pledged allegiance to? To them, the Christian life could be marked by a surgical procedure and a rule book. Sounds foolish to us, but I wonder if the circumcision party is alive and well in our hearts. Do we mark a believer by his *style* of worship, or by his *life* of worship? Do raised hands signify true spirituality to us? Do hands not raised mark someone as a non-worshiper?

How about an example that's a little less churchy? Is a Christian marked by his preference in music? Many Christians cannot see Jesus in contemporary Christian music because the musicians don't follow an unwritten code of Christian rules. Like the circumcision party, these people insist the singers bear external marks of a certain brand of Christianity. Instead, the musicians prefer to live according to the Spirit, allowing attitudes, actions, and words to give a unique expression of Jesus to a lost world.

The point is, we are not governed by a rule book of Christian living. Before Christ, the rule book served as our baby-sitter. We were immature, needing someone to watch over us but resenting it miserably. "The heir, as long as he is a child, is no better than a slave, though he is the owner of all the estate; but he is under guardians and trustees until the date set by the father" (4:1-2).

Unfortunately, we all find points of legalism in our lives at times. We can be like a wealthy child, unable to handle his money. He needs others to manage his affairs for him. The legalist must have his baby-sitter, the Law, with him at all times. The riches of a daily walk with Christ are not realized.

This could also be thought of in terms of a rich man with amnesia. He forgets about all the money stashed in his bank account. He only sees bills being sent through the mail, and he struggles to pay them. The legalistic

Christian struggles to meet external demands in his own strength, not drawing from his only real Power for living.

Paul wanted his Galatian friends to understand that they were trying to do something which they were actually unable to do. As the wealthy child who is unable to manage his money, so the legalist is unable to live the Christian life in his own strength. By stressing their own need to keep the Law, the Galatians returned to the bondage of being lost children.

"So with us; when we were children, we were slaves to the elemental spirits of the universe" (v. 3). Paul's use of pronouns (*us, we*) showed that he included himself in this group. He compared the legalistic life he lived with the Galatians' pre-Christ days of idolatry. Both were without Christ; both were lost children.

The continual reference to lost people as "children" makes one think of a child separated from his parents inside a large shopping mall. Few things are more traumatic for a young child. This is the legalist's state of being; out of touch with his Father, he blindly struggles down unknown aisles with only his own wisdom to guide him.

As in chapter three, Paul compared the life of a legalist to witchcraft. The "elemental spirits of the universe" are considered by many scholars to be the mystery religions of Paul's day. An adherent to such a religion would consult mediums, attend secret mysterious meetings (like seances), and check out astrological charts to determine his destiny.

Such godlessness compares to the legalist who actually thinks he can determine his destiny by acts of his own will. Both types of godlessness are, in fact, bondage. By embracing the Law, the Galatians took on another form of bondage. As their mystery religions couldn't save them, neither could their new religious observances. Only the Jesus who clothed them in righteousness could be their life-giving empowerment.

In every religious movement, man controls his destiny through his own willpower. In Christianity, God controls the destiny of the believer. Islam is a very real threat in our world. Based on Old Testament principles, it challenges Christianity as the other major "revealed religion." It preaches a gospel of works and powerless living guided by human willpower submitted to Allah. Christians can counter this and every other religious persuasion by displaying power-filled lives of faith.

We must be extremely careful not to heap rules and regulations on believers. Doing so will reduce the Christian faith to a religion based on man working his way to God. God has done a great work on the Cross to bring man to Himself. Our faith is God's idea, motivated by God's desire, and infused with God's power.

"But when the time had fully come, God sent forth his Son, born of woman, born under the law" (v. 4). Here again, God steps into history. History can be seen at a world level (including the entire human race) and at a personal level. God controls both the history of the world and the history of each of His people. Remember, the word *but* marks the change from godlessness to godliness. Earlier in this letter, we saw that *but* served as the turning point in Paul's personal life (1:15). Here we see the word *but* serve as the turning point of the world. The birth of Jesus into the world marks the most significant period in history; all of history is dated from that event.

The greatest moment in any believer's life is the time when Christ stepped in. Each year, Christmas celebrates the fact that God came into the world. In the same way, each Christian can view the time when Christ stepped into his life as the greatest reason to celebrate. Some Christians celebrate their spiritual birthday every year by giving gifts to friends and having a party. For them, this celebration is as important as Christmas. The birth of Christ into the world is meaningless for an individual if it's not applied personally.

Notice the fact that Jesus was "born under the law" (v. 4). Jesus is our substitute in His life as well as in His death. He was the only man to ever give complete obedience to the Law, but He came from heaven to be more than an example to us. He lived a life of perfection, and therefore at death became a perfect sacrifice. Through our faith, God places the obedience of Christ onto the accounts of undeserving, disobedient believers.

Almost everyone recognizes Jesus as a "great teacher." Scribes and Pharisees saw him as such, as do today's Hindus, Buddhists, Muslims, and humanists. The circumcision party would also have seen Him as a great teacher. They probably tried to emulate His life, being obedient to the Law.

Much more than just a "good example," Jesus is our substitute and our enabler. He is not to be seen as "One of the great legends who has gone before us" as though He belongs in the "Religious Leaders Hall of Fame." Jesus is the only reason we can live lives pleasing to God. His life's mission was to "redeem those who were under the law, so that we might receive adoption as sons" (v. 5). The word *redeem* comes from the Greek slave markets. One could redeem a slave by buying him out of his slavery, never to be sold as a slave again. Jesus went to the slave market of sin and bought us, using His own blood as payment (I Peter 1:18).

Not only did He redeem us from slavery, He adopted us into His family. To Galatians of the first century, adoption meant a change of identity and name, and a cancellation of debts. With the former life of bondage out of the way, an entirely new life of freedom could begin.

Today's process of child adoption is often long and difficult. Some couples wait for years before becoming eligible; some wait their entire lives. Adoption agencies are strict in order to protect children from potential dangers. The dangers are greater than just having "unsuitable parents." Adopted children also risk being sold into the black market, where they would be used for illegal, abusive activities (such as child pornography).

We were once spiritual black-market babies, sold into sin, governed by our master, the Law. God removed us from the black market, making us into His own sons. No longer held in bondage to a life of sin, we enjoy all the rights and privileges of sonship. We have the inheritance of our Father—personal righteousness.

"And because you are sons, God has sent the Spirit of his Son into our hearts, crying 'Abba! Father!'" (v. 6) *Abba* is an intimate Aramaic word, used by a child when speaking informally to his father (e.g., *Daddy*). A true son of God relates to God as father. Although the circumcision party, as good Jews, understood God to be the father of their race, they lacked the father/son relationship with Him.

"So through God you are no longer a slave but a son, and if a son then an heir" (v. 7). The Galatians had been given all the rights and privileges of sons of God. Through Jesus, they could have direct access to the Father. The old baby-sitter who filled in for the true Parent was no longer needed.

Why would they prefer the baby-sitter? This is a good question; one which has no logical or biblical answer. Yet many Christians do find it more convenient to control their own lives through dead rules rather than allow God full reign. "Backslider" defines someone who turns away from the simple Gospel of grace to live in his old lifestyle. And legalism is merely backsliding in a fancy package.

Questions, Review, and Interpretation

1. How did the Galatians' initial salvation experience differ from their present experience?

2. How is Jesus both a blessing and a curse?

3. What does it mean to be a son of Abraham?

4. What are the purposes of the Old Testament Law?

5. What is the significance of the word *custodian*? What is the significance of the word *offspring*?

Application:

1. In considering your Christian experience, have you grown stale in any way? If so, how?

2. What characteristics of Abraham should be in your life to show that you are his spiritual descendent?

3. What are the reasons that you are qualified to receive God's blessing?

4. What were/are some of the ways that made/make you realize how short you fall of God's glory?

5. What are the things which qualify Jesus to be your Redeemer? How should this affect your thinking in relation to God?

11

Taking Back the Chains

Formerly, when you did not know God, you were in bondage to beings that by nature are no gods; but now that you have come to know God, or rather to be known by God, how can you turn back again to the weak and beggarly elemental spirits, whose slaves you want to be once more? You observe days, and months, and seasons, and years! I am afraid I have labored over you in vain.

Brethren, I beseech you, become as I am, for I also have become as you are. You did me no wrong; you know it was because of a bodily ailment that I preached the gospel to you at first; and though my condition was a trial to you, you did not scorn or despise me, but received me as an angel of God, as Christ Jesus. What has become of the satisfaction you felt? For I bear you witness that, if possible, you would have plucked out your eyes and given them to me. Have I then become your enemy by telling you the truth? They make much of you, but for no good purpose; they want to shut you out, that you may make much of them. For a good purpose it is always good to be made much of, and not only when I am present with you. My little children, with whom I am again in travail until Christ be formed

in you! I could wish to be present with you now and to
change my tone, for I am perplexed about you.
                                                   Galatians 4:8-20

It is time again for the legalistic Galatians to apply
Paul's message. His theology and clever illustrations
have painted a clear picture of their own lives. God had
done a mighty work of grace for them, in that through
Jesus they had become sons of God, freed from a harsh
baby-sitter. By rejecting the simple Gospel of faith in
Christ, the Galatians pledged allegiance to the Law, the
cruel master who had condemned them.

This passage highlights Paul's heart of love for these
young believers. He longed that Christ be formed in them;
he grieved over their wandering from the truth. Their
deviation from God had also affected their relationship
with Paul. Reducing the Christian faith to a mere rule
book not only damages one's relationship with God, but
it also severs bonds within the Body of Christ.

Paul invited the Galatians to walk with him down
memory lane. "Formerly, when you did not know God,
you were in bondage to beings that by nature are no gods"
(v. 8). He reminds them of the "good old days" of bondage
and slavery, when their lives were weighed down with
heavy burdens. It is rare that a freed prisoner lies awake
at night, longing for the cold, lonely cell that he once
called home. Certainly the Galatians had not recognized
their new prison house as the one which had previously
held them captive. Their present cell-keeper, the Law,
seemed far different from their prior guard, the mystery
religions. Although one appeared much more "clean-cut"
than the other, the two were actually twin brothers. Paul
described both as "weak and beggarly elemental spirits"
(v. 9). The mystery religions which the Galatians had
known, and the Law which the circumcision party exalted, were both avenues for a bondage seeker to tread.
The pursuit of either was a man-made attempt at righ-

teousness, and both created slaves.

Legalistic Christians should be challenged to remember the simple saving faith that allowed them to first see God. Those who live the Christian life by "principle" rather than by the Spirit are no more free than they were in their days of sensual pleasure. They may be clean shaven and use nicer words, but their hearts are equally as bound.

By observing days, months, seasons, and years (v. 10), the Galatians had merely substituted Jewish feasts for Gentile ones. God gets no big thrill out of festivals. A Chinese person who celebrates Christmas instead of his Moon Festival is not made any more commendable to God, because activities are not a sufficient base for righteousness. Of course, few sincere Christians would say that going to church means they are a step closer to heaven. But I wonder how many would feel guilty—unacceptable to God—if they missed church. We go to church to commune with God and His family. Activities, observing days, and doing works are not grounds for approaching God. We approach Him because He has adopted us into sonship.

The Galatians had gotten to "know God" and to "be known by God" (v. 9). They are asked to remember God's election. As God had stepped into Paul's life (1:15) and into history (4:4), so He came to them and chose them. Not only do they "know God," through Christ they are intimately known by the God of the universe.

People often become enthralled over big names. If we've ever met a famous personality, we would probably say, "I know him, but I'm sure he doesn't know me." God is the world's most famous Personality (Romans 1 says that everyone realizes He is there), and He introduced Himself to us before we even had a chance to ask for His autograph.

The Galatians gave away a personal relationship with

God and, instead, embraced religious activities. Their attitude was the same as Christians who say, "I don't have time to spend with God. I have to go to church." A farmer would follow the same line of thinking by ignoring his cattle or crops to build a barn. The very heart of one's occupation is forgotten for secondary activities. It's no wonder that Paul would feel like all his efforts were in vain (v. 11). The Galatians returned to a bondage just as heavy as that from which he had pointed them. He would certainly feel all his work had been for nothing.

I know it seems we've said this many times before, and we have. Paul was trying to make a point, and we need to hear it.

Some missionary friends in Hong Kong work with a group of people called "street sleepers." These homeless "down-and-outers" are usually unemployed, often addicted to hard drugs, living their lives from meal to meal. The missionaries invite them into a halfway house, provide for them, share the Gospel with them, and teach them how to function in society. Often, just weeks after they leave the halfway house, these people are back on the streets again, willingly returning to empty lives of bondage. Of course, our friends sometimes begin to think their many hours of work amount to nothing.

In the same way, Paul felt that all his evangelistic efforts were in vain. And if Paul, the mere preacher, felt this way, how do you think Jesus, the actual Message, felt? His work on the Cross had enabled these Galatians to receive adoption into sonship. By returning to bondage, they neglected both His obedient life and His passionate death—the entire scope of the work which He had done for them.

As Christ certainly still loves them, so Paul, Christ's messenger, is not bearing a grudge. Love brought him to Galatia in the first place—love for them and love for the Gospel. The Galatians were asked to remember not only their salvation experience, but also their initial meeting of an adventuresome apostle. Like an old married couple urged to remember and rekindle their youthful love for each other, so the Galatians were asked to recall their days with Paul. He had somehow ended up on their doorstep in need of medical attention (v. 13). No one really knows what ailed Paul. All kinds of diseases are guessed at, from trachoma to malaria.

Anyway, the Galatians had met him with warm hospitality. The statement, "You would have plucked out your eyes and given them to me," doesn't necessarily imply that Paul had eye problems. We could possibly replace it with an English saying, "You would have given me the shirt off your back." The point is, the Galatians had been very kind to him, in spite of his poor reception by their Jewish countrymen (Acts 14). They didn't care for him simply because they wanted to side with the one being picked on by Jewish bullies. They had received Paul as a messenger (angel) of God, as Christ Jesus Himself (v. 14). The fact that Paul brought them the Gospel—their own deliverance—caused them to treat him with all the honor shown to the lifeguard who rescues a drowning swimmer.

Paul argues against their return to the swirling pools of heresy. "Become as I am, for I also have become as you are (v. 12). In a way, he had become as they were, free from the Law of Moses. Those rules to which he had so rigidly adhered were dropped for something (i.e., Someone) better. The Galatians had dug up the very thing Paul had buried, and he asked them to bury again that self-righteousness, worth about as much as garbage. Christians should have a "self-righteousness garbage pile," where dead works can be either buried or burned, whichever analogy is most destructive.

It is understandably ironic to Paul that the very message which endeared him to the Galatians should now make him an enemy (v. 16). Obviously, the circumcision party had raked his name through some legalistic mud. In the process, they not only dirtied the name of an apostle, but even worse, they stained the simple, pure Gospel.

Paul utterly disassociated himself from the circumcision party (v. 17). If by some chance the Galatians had any confusion over these two ministries, Paul cleared the air. *They* were not seeking the welfare of his children in Christ (v. 17). *They* might have appeared very loving and up-building but were actually wolves in sheep's clothing.

By then, the Galatians may have felt that Paul was just being defensive. Was he feeling left out, like the kid whose idea gets rejected by the gang? Actually, Paul sincerely wanted the best for his spiritual children, whether that "best" was received from his hand or from the hand of another (v. 18). The point was that the circumcision party was giving them the worst—bondage to the Law.

Such rules "shut out" believers from the blessing of Christ (v. 17). In sports, a team is shut out when they fail to score a goal. So the Galatians failed to receive power, life, and love from God because they became consumed with rule-keeping and working from their own limited power, life, and love. As the Galatians were shut out, the circumcision party was "made much of" (v. 17). As the most practiced rule-keepers, the circumcision party sought approval for their discipline and "godliness."

Even though they had rejected Paul's message, the Galatians were still his "little children" (v. 19). Such long-suffering love fills a committed pastor's heart for his flock. The one who teaches the way to spiritual birth is just as significant as the one who gives physical birth. Paul could truly be called their "father." Paul's travail over his flock's spiritual condition could be compared to birth pains. The Galatians had regressed to a place of spiritual immaturity, needing to be spoon-fed with the rules of childish religion. He longed that they bear the only mark of Christian maturity: Jesus.

Did the Galatians need to be "born again" again? No, the one new birth is sufficient for a new creation. But Paul's hope was that Christ be formed in them and that their Christian character would reflect the Person of Jesus rather than a written set of rules. So they didn't need to re-experience justification, the time when God declared them righteous. But they did need to continually experience another aspect of salvation: sanctification.

Sanctification means to grow in the experience of holiness. Chapters five and six detail some marks of the sanctified life. These relate to the Holy Spirit's life being reflected through a believer. If a person has known an original experience and touch by the Holy Spirit, their lives should reflect *holy* qualities. The Galatians covered up this life with self-effort, working from human strength rather than the strength of the Spirit.

Think of the sanctified believer as a drinking glass, and the Holy Spirit as deep red tomato juice. Pour tomato juice in the glass, and it becomes red. Everyone can plainly see tomato juice in the glass. The legalistic believer is more like a ceramic mug. Pour tomato juice in the mug, and the contents are hidden behind a ceramic exterior. In the same way, the Holy Spirit is not seen behind the rules of a legalistic believer.

The Galatians covered up the Holy Spirit with circumcision and other laws. Do people see the vibrant life of the Holy Spirit when they look at us? Or do they see "religion"—someone attempting to live a rigid, principled life? It may shock us to realize that the God we want to make known is sometimes covered up behind our good works. And the simple Gospel becomes lost in a list of do's and don'ts.

12

Now for a Look at Mother

Tell me, you who desire to be under law, do you not hear the law? For it is written that Abraham had two sons, one by a slave and one by a free woman. But the son of the slave was born according to the flesh, the son of the free woman through promise. Now this is an allegory: these women are two covenants. One is from Mount Sinai, bearing children for slavery; she is Hagar. Now Hagar is Mount Sinai in Arabia; she corresponds to the present Jerusalem, for she is in slavery with her children. But the Jerusalem above is free, and she is our mother. For it is written, "Rejoice, O barren one that dost not bear; break forth and shout, thou who art not in travail; for the desolate hath more children than she who hath a husband."

Now we, brethren, like Isaac, are children of promise. But as at that time he who was born according to the flesh persecuted him who was born according to the Spirit, so it is now. But what does the scripture say? "Cast out the slave and her son; for the son of the slave shall not inherit with the son of the free woman." So, brethren, we are not children of the slave but of the free woman.

Galatians 4:21-31

We are nearing the end of Paul's history/theology lesson. By now you've noticed that his message is draped in a family-type package. So far, we have met the father of faith, Abraham, as well as the hired baby-sitter, the Law. Now it's time to meet the mother.

Before we do that, let's notice Paul's tone in this passage. Whereas the previous paragraph in Galatians was tinged with sentimental thoughts, he now returns to the attack. The Galatians are falling into harmful doctrinal error and require a swift kick in their theology.

Paul was not schizophrenic, alternating his letter with "I love you" and "I hate you." He was more like a father who sees his child ruining his life with drugs. Where anger over a devastating habit may appear unloving, the father's anger is actually motivated by love. In the same way, love for his flock motivated Paul's harsh rebukes of their fall from grace. Here he delivered another lesson from the Law, the set of books which the circumcision party exalted. *The Law* actually refers to the Pentateuch, or the first five books of the Bible. From these, Paul drew all his historical arguments. Those who wanted to live under the Law actually deleted much of it (v. 21).

This lesson on "spiritual motherhood" is taken from Genesis and concerns two women, Sarah and Hagar. At first glance, we may feel that Paul twisted Scripture to make his point. Actually, his argument was very sound, although very offensive to the Jews.

It's important to note the use of contrast in this passage. Contrast is a writer's tool which highlights a point by stating its opposite. The best way for someone to appear thin is to stand beside a very obese person. In the same way, Paul highlighted freedom in Christ by placing that concept next to bondage to the Law.

Here he made thorough use of contrast, relating several opposites to these two famous ladies.

The following list highlights these contrasts:

Hagar	Sarah
1. slave	1. free woman
2. Ishmael	2. Isaac
3. flesh	3. promise
4. bears children for slavery	4. mother of the free
5. present Jerusalem	5. Jerusalem above
6. cast out	6. heirs

"Abraham had two sons, one by a slave and one by a free woman" (v. 22). Every good Sunday school student will know that these two sons were called Ishmael and Isaac. Scripture has very little good to say about the first boy. Before his birth, God had already known that Ishmael would be like "a wild ass of a man, his hand against every man and every man's hand against him" (Gen. 16:12). Isaac, on the other hand, is summarized in Scripture by one word: *promise*. He was a little boy promised to doubting parents, people who laughed at God's "ridiculous" word.

We know Abraham took God's promise into his own hands and produced Ishmael, an unacceptable work of the flesh. This happened during a low ebb in the faith of the Hebrew couple. Rather than trusting God to do a miracle in an impossible situation, they strove to "get" God's promise. They tried to present something to God of their own merit; a child born by their own ingenuity. Abraham tried to "flesh" his way into God's presence.

Of course, *flesh* doesn't refer to the physical body. Isaac appeared through physical childbirth in a very normal way. (Except that his mother was 90 years old.) In saying that Ishmael's birth was "according to the flesh," Paul means that God wasn't involved. Isaac's birth, on the other hand, had no explanation apart from God's intervention. He was God's promise, believed and received by two special people.

The circumcision party neglected such promises. They "fleshed" their way to God by doing some things they thought would please the "Rich Old Guy in the Sky." Push-button Christianity—which treats God flippantly—governed their lives. "We get circumcised, God blesses us; we keep the Sabbath, God blesses us...." So they denied the faith of their physical father and mother, Abraham and Sarah.

Paul said their lives could more easily be compared to Hagar's. Now he was becoming offensive. If any loyal Jews, such as the circumcision party, were still reading this controversial letter, they were probably either convicted or upset. In the next verses Paul seemed to slight Jewish history, the source of pride for most Hebrews. Actually, he denounced Jewish bondage, not history.

Rabbis loved to listen to interpretations of their holy Law, but most would not have appreciated Paul's. To label such an important part of their history with the term *allegory* would seem like very poor exegesis (not to mention being extremely unkind). But Paul was not really making Jewish history into an allegory. He was actually going to the very origin of Jewish history, a starting place even prior to Abraham.

Hagar and Sarah are the two main characters in this story, representing two points of origin. Paul's aim in using this Old Testament illustration was this: Hagar bore a child in an earthly, natural way; Sarah bore a child by heavenly, spiritual means. Hagar's children are fleshly, Sarah's children, spiritual. So, two origins are possible—heaven or earth.

Most Jews would have no problem with the association of the terms *slavery, flesh, Arabia* with Hagar. In fact, they probably applauded these word associations. But how could Paul connect Mt. Sinai (the place where God gave the Law to their Jewish forefathers) with Abraham's mistake? And Jerusalem, the city of God? Such a shame that Paul would destroy his good arguments with far-fetched interpretation.

Paul's point was this: Jerusalem was no more special than any other place. Those Jews who exalted the Jerusalem church as "mother church" were getting a lesson on spiritual motherhood. And some would be surprised to discover that they were actually illegitimate children.

By now, we've gotten the point of this passage. Placing one's confidence in human, physical things (such as the "Law" or "Jerusalem") is unacceptable to God. By waving our good works in God's face, we place ourselves in the category of Hagar, the slave.

The circumcision party would certainly have become upset by Paul's words about the present Jerusalem (v. 25). They had insisted these Galatians submit to the "mother church," because it existed in the "Holy City." To Paul, such thinking was flesh-centered, from unheavenly sources. The heavenly Jerusalem is free; and it is the Galatians' frame of reference.

This heavenly Jerusalem refers to children born of Sarah. As Paul's quotation from Isaiah shows (v. 27), her children are many more than those of Hagar. (Notice that by using this quotation, Paul refers to Hagar as the "married" one. This should be understood as meaning the one who had children in a natural way.) Sarah's "many more" children include those Gentiles (the Galatians and us) who have received adoption into God's family through faith. As was Isaac, we are "heirs according to promise."

The entire point of this passage was to state the origin of God's true children. "Now we, brethren, like Isaac, are children of promise" (v. 28). Most of us cannot claim to be direct descendants of Abraham, but as Isaac was born supernaturally, by God's promise, so we are born supernaturally by the Spirit of God. Only Sarah bore children in the promised line, because she bore children of promise. As God's grace prevailed over her unbelieving laughter (Gen. 18:11-15), so His grace has prevailed over our own unworthy, sinful hearts. We are children of promise.

However, our only ground for being called "children of promise," "God's sons" or "God's daughters," is faith in the Person and Work of Jesus.

Jesus made the same distinction in John chapter eight. As he confronted Jews who were proud of their physical descent from Abraham, Jesus told them of their true origin. "You are of your father the devil, and your will is to do your father's desires" (John 8:44). His statement about the origin of legalism was even more descriptive than Paul's. As the devil lives to exalt himself, so legalists live to honor their own self-righteous abilities. Remember, legalism is comparable to witchcraft.

Now that Paul had shown the identities of Sarah's true children, he stated two of their characteristics: suffering and inheriting. As Ishmael persecuted Isaac (Gen. 21:9; NIV or KJV), so the descendants of Ishmael (the circumcision party) persecute the descendants of Isaac (children of promise). Like a prisoner who resents his cellmate's release, so legalistic Christians are bothered by the freedom of other Christians. The circumcision party is somewhat alive and well in our church today, and quite possibly breathes inside our own hearts.

For example, the circumcision party of today's church may say that only those with university degrees are fit to minister. In their eyes, a piece of paper means as much as, or more than, the call of God. Such slavery deserves to be cast out (v. 30). Not only does the circumcision party persecute, but it has no place in God's kingdom. External qualifications are not grounds for receiving an inheritance. The inheritance is given to legitimate sons made heirs through Jesus. We are not denying the value of formal education. In God's leading, it is of immense value, but it is not necessarily a prerequisite for ministry. And it cannot possibly make one a better son of God.

We are sons of God through faith. All the history and theology of chapters three and four have shown this to be true. The basis of our sonship is God's own goodness—the fact that He has adopted us into His family because of His grace. As sons, we can approach our Father freely. A father will always recognize his own son, since the marks of sonship are obvious on the boy's face, body, and actions. But so often, Christians feel like God won't recognize them unless they first prove their sonship. Sadly enough, their proof often consists of their own good works—Bible reading, church attendance, helping others—rather than God's grace. Unless they do these, they feel ashamed to approach God.

The Father looks for a more important mark of identification: righteousness through Jesus. He accepts the son who can honestly say, "I have no reason for being here in your presence other than the fact that You have given me life." The Father waits for His children, and accepts us just the way we are.

Questions, Review, and Interpretation

1. What are "weak and beggarly elemental spirits"?

2. How were the false teachers making much of the Galatians? How would the Galatians have made much of them?

3. Why does Paul treat the Hagar/Sarah story as an allegory?

4. What is the "Jerusalem above"?

5. From Galatians chapter four, summarize Paul's feelings for the Galatian believers.

Application:

1. What attitudes would you bury or burn on your "self-righteousness garbage pile"?

2. To what are you in danger of becoming a slave?

3. What are some aspects of Christian lifestyle or attitude that would befit a child of Hagar?

4. Can you think of any ways that you have tried to "flesh" your way to God?

5. Do your beliefs or good works *cause* or *feed* your pride? If so, ask yourself if these are products of your flesh.

Part Five

The Practice of Grace:
Free to be Servants

13

Using an Expired ID

For freedom Christ has set us free; stand fast therefore, and do not submit again to a yoke of slavery.

Now I, Paul, say to you that if you receive circumcision, Christ will be of no advantage to you. I testify again to every man who receives circumcision that he is bound to keep the whole law. You are severed from Christ, you who would be justified by the law; you have fallen away from grace. For through the Spirit, by faith, we wait for the hope of righteousness. For in Christ Jesus neither circumcision nor uncircumcision is of any avail, but faith working through love. You were running well; who hindered you from obeying the truth? This persuasion is not from him who called you. A little leaven leavens the whole lump. I have confidence in the Lord that you will take no other view than mine; and he who is troubling you will bear his judgment, whoever he is. But if I, brethren, still preach circumcision, why am I still persecuted? In that case the stumbling block of the cross has been removed. I wish those who unsettle you would mutilate themselves!

Galatians 5:1-12

A missionary friend once took his passport from his drawer, looked inside, and noticed that his visa had expired months earlier. He felt sick as he considered what the authorities might do to him. His expired "ID" gave him no right to be in their country. (Fortunately, after paying a small fine, the situation was rectified and he was allowed to stay.)

These next two chapters of Galatians reveal the Christian's true identification marks. His badge is not circumcision or some other outdated set of rituals. The Christian is identified by a Christ-centered, Cross-centered life. Only a believer who carries the Cross has the correct "ID" for being in God's presence.

The practice of grace, the "how-to's" of the Christian life, appear at the end of this letter to the Galatians. Does that mean ethics are unimportant? No, it merely points to their origin. Right living marks every sincere child of God, but as the unfolding plot of Paul's letter shows, the person who lives right must first be a child of God.

So far in Galatians, we have learned that the father has much to do with his son. First, the son comes into being through the actions of his father. In the same way, we are sons of God because of His gracious work done for us through Jesus. Now Paul says that the father should give his son a good example of how to live. Our good works must always be explained by the fact that Jesus did a good work first.

"For freedom Christ has set us free; stand fast therefore, and do not submit again to a yoke of slavery" (v. 1). This verse sums up everything Paul has already said. It also serves as the basis for the following section on right living. Christ has freed us from our prisons—the bondage of trying to please God through self-effort. That freedom should always be obvious in our lives.

The word *stand* is important in this section. People guided by restless hearts don't usually like the idea of "staying put." The simplicity of the Cross seems too simple to be a base for one's entire life. The restless heart of a Christian often screams, "Let's move on to bigger and better things." Especially in this "new age," the hunt is on for "new truths" to help our hurting world.

The work of Christ on the Cross is the biggest and best thing that's ever happened to mankind. The Christian life must be lived with the Cross as its reference point. When that ceases to be the focal point of a church or of one's individual experience, one will quickly move into un-biblical "tangent" living.

For the Galatians, the tangent was circumcision. With a cut of the knife, they made a very definite statement: I am now good enough for God. By emphasizing a work, the Galatians de-emphasized Christ's finished work. And they treated God like a fraternity leader, someone who requires new members be put through a painful initiation ceremony.

Of course, circumcision has not been an issue in the Church for years. But as we've explained throughout this book, the circumcision-party mentality has always been with us in very subtle (and not so subtle) ways. Throughout history, Christians have done a strange variety of things in their attempts at being made more commendable to God.

Simon Stylites lived as a monk in the fifth century. As part of a group known as the "athletes for God," he and his friends punished themselves ruthlessly in order to gain God's acceptance. Simon did such amazing stunts as touching his feet to his forehead 1,244 times in succession, and living on top of a small pillar for 36 years. One wonders if God laughed or cried in response.

Today in some nations, there are so-called Christians who celebrate Easter by crucifying themselves. They think that God was so pleased with sending Jesus to the Cross that He'll be especially tickled if they do the same. Martin Luther lived a vigorous life of self-inflicted misery before the Reformation. He discovered that his days of fasting, praying "overtime," and spending multiplied hours in public confession were an insufficient basis for being accepted by God.

In most churches today, we would easily recognize and avoid such extreme legalism. But do we talk about "living a principled life" more than about "Christ's death for unworthy sinners"? *Standing* means to stay put, to not progress past the simple message that saved us. A little girl is told to stand still, wait for her parents, and to not take any rides from strangers. A Christian must always remain at the foot of the Cross in order to not be carried off by strange, man-inspired teaching.

"If you receive circumcision, Christ will be of no advantage to you" (v. 2). The Christian must choose how he will live the Christian life. Either Jesus is the reason for His salvation, or self-effort is a good enough ticket into God's throne room. The Galatians are asked to make a decision on how they will live: by Christ or by works. Oh, by the way...if they choose works, they will be "bound to keep the whole law" (v. 3).

The circumcision ritual provides a nice illustration for the legalist's separation from Christ. The Galatian who depends on circumcision for salvation cuts off more than just a piece of skin. He actually severs his entire relationship with Christ. Why? Because he's made a statement that Jesus isn't enough for his salvation. The Christian who looks to his own works for justification has "fallen away from grace" (v. 4).

Since Paul made this statement more than 1,900 years ago, the church has been divided over a deep theological question: Is it possible for a born-again believer to lose his salvation? This is not the place to dive into such heated pools of controversy.

This is where Christian freedom comes in. Some go to movies, some don't. Some adhere to strict dress codes, some don't. It is imperative that these different groups honor each other and go out of their way not to offend each other.

Primarily, Paul is not setting forth a statement on eternal security. Rather, he's giving his friends some shocking news about their spiritual programs.

That which they had hoped would draw them closer to God actually moved them away from Him. "Falling away from grace" equals the concept of "apostasy" described in the letter to the Hebrews. The author of that epistle also writes to a group of people who have misplaced their trust. Rather than relying on Christ's work, they had decided to trust in their own efforts under the Law of Moses.

How does this apply to us? Few Christians say that keeping the Law of Moses draws them closer to God. But many trust in spiritual programs rather than trusting Christ alone for righteousness.

We sometimes tend to view God as an Olympic judge, one who watches our performance and rates us accordingly. The one who stumbles during competition may expect the shame of a very low score. As dishonest athletes inflate themselves with steroids, so legalistic Christians major on the external forms of the faith. Such fabricated strength helps their routine look better and gives an appearance of strength. But what happens to the athlete caught using steroids? He's eliminated from the competition. The Christian who relies on external marks of "Christianity" in order to please the Judge is filled with spiritual steroids. He disqualifies himself from the race set before him.

Through the Spirit, we have been given power to live better lives. But as explained earlier, this world is far from "glory land." Throughout the New Testament, believers are encouraged to wait for something better. Inner transformation through the Spirit is only a foretaste of a glorious future. In Titus 2:11-13, Paul explains well the concept of "living and waiting": "For the grace of God has appeared for the salvation of all men, training us to renounce irreligion and worldly passions, and to live sober, upright, and godly lives in this world, awaiting our blessed hope, the appearing of the glory of our great God and Savior Jesus Christ."

The grace of God helps us to live the Christian life here on earth and to wait for Christ's return from heaven. Legalism, on the other hand, distorts not only the present life but also the future hope. With an over-concern on external programs and rituals, the legalist removes his eyes from Christ, his ultimate hope. His mind becomes fixed on the present world, on his own self-sanctification.

"In Christ Jesus neither circumcision nor uncircumcision is of any avail, but faith working through love" (v. 6). To Paul, Jewish observances were non-issues. The entire point of this letter was to show that man is made free through Christ. The main issue in our faith should be worded, "Am I trusting in Christ?" not "Am I doing all the right things?" Only when a person takes rituals upon himself as a means of commending himself to God (i.e., self-righteousness) do these become an issue.

Circumcision neither helped nor hurt one's standing with God. Remember earlier in this letter we learned that Paul did not circumcise Titus (2:3). However, in Acts we learned that he did circumcise another disciple, Timothy (Acts 16:1-3). In both of these situations, each handled differently, he was making a point: only faith working through love is of importance to the Christian.

By not circumcising Titus, Paul highlighted the faith aspect. His message to the legalists is clear: faith in Christ, not faith in rituals, can save a sinner. By circumcising Timothy, Paul didn't change his message; he merely highlighted the love aspect. Love for the Jews, a desire for them to know God, caused him to circumcise this disciple. He would even stoop to their unenlightened level in order to see them saved. He became "all things to all men, that he might win some."

"You were running well; who hindered you from obeying the truth?" (v. 7) The Christian is hindered when his eyes are removed from Christ. Obedience to the truth is not comprised of living by all the right principles. Rather, obedience involves keeping one's eyes on Jesus, the means of God's grace.

The writer to the Hebrews challenges us to "run with perseverance the race set before us, looking to Jesus, the pioneer and perfecter of our faith" (Heb. 12:1,2). The Christian life may be compared to a long-distance race. Jesus is the goal, and the Christian runs through life, always keeping Him clearly in sight.

A long-distance runner does not stop at various points in the race to run down other paths. He stays on one path, with one goal in sight. The Galatians dropped out of the race to pursue other paths. "This persuasion is not from him who calls you" (v. 8). By not keeping sight of Jesus, their goal, the Galatians followed after some misguided runners. The circumcision party drew them away from Christ into minor issues.

It only takes one misguided runner to lead others astray (v. 9). Each person in the race must keep the goal, Jesus, in sight. When we follow after others, we can never really be sure they are running down the correct path. The history of the Church is full of stories about Christians who have followed people, thinking these leaders would point them to Christ. Thank God for men like the apostle Paul and Martin Luther, men who have moved their eyes from fallible human beings to infallible Jesus.

Our eyes must always be on Christ, the hope of righteousness. He alone is central to the Christian faith. Christian programs must keep Christ central, for everything else is secondary. Paul was utterly convinced of this. His assurance may have appeared narrow-minded because he basically said, "Either agree with my letter or God will judge you" (v. 10). Unlike some in the "watered-down" twentieth-century church, Paul left no room for opposing views on such a major issue. We also must leave no room for secondary issues to become central issues. When programs, principles, or any "good" thing receives higher priority than the work of Christ, we must bring in the correct emphasis. Paul sees the Galatians' salvation as well worth fighting for. The Gospel is God's power for salvation to everyone who believes. Any emphasis in the Church which is over and above the simple Gospel must be brought under the Cross.

The "stumbling block of the cross" is also part of life's race (v. 11). The phrase *stumbling block* in Greek actually means "trap" or "snare." Legalists get carried down the wrong path by failing to see the Cross as their direction in life. They fall into a trap of self-righteousness by avoiding the only means to righteousness.

Why do they avoid the Cross? For one thing, the way of the Cross is not easy—simple, maybe, but not easy. To the religious-minded Jew, the Cross meant they would have to die to their nice religious ceremonies. These rituals, although once good in that they pointed to Jesus, had come to the point of stressing more human strength. Not only personal ego-boosters, these also could look very good to outside observers.

Paul received persecution for living by the Cross. Jesus promised that the way of the Cross would not be easy (Mark 8:35). The Cross says something which mankind finds very insulting: people can do nothing to save themselves. This is the message by which we live. The Cross speaks death to all acts of self-righteousness.

Paul's words to those who preached a contrary message would not place him in the "Top Ten of Social Etiquette." "I wish those who unsettle you would mutilate themselves!" (v. 12) Our English translations tone this statement down quite a bit. His words almost certainly meant, "I wish those who practice circumcision would go all the way and castrate themselves." To us, such words may appear unloving, perhaps even childishly vindictive. Actually, Paul loved his friends so much that he anguished over the thought of their harm. Those who hurt them were destroyers who should be destroyed themselves.

On a physical level, we would probably share the same negative thoughts for a suicide bomber. His explosives will certainly destroy him in the process of his attempted murder. We can only hope they would detonate before he had the chance to harm innocent people.

In the same way, the circumcision party was hindering the Galatians' Christian walk. They must be opposed. A true Christian bears far more important marks of identification. His crucifixion—that is, death to self—is one obvious mark. But as the next chapter shows, even more evident is his new life, lived through the Holy Spirit's power.

14

The Living Walk of a Dead Man

For you were called to freedom, brethren; only do not use your freedom as an opportunity for the flesh, but through love be servants of one another. For the whole Law is fulfilled in one word, "You shall love your neighbor as yourself." But if you bite and devour one another take heed that you are not consumed by one another.

But I say, walk by the Spirit, and do not gratify the desires of the flesh. For the desires of the flesh are against the Spirit, and the desires of the Spirit are against the flesh; for these are opposed to each other, to prevent you from doing what you would. But if you are led by the Spirit you are not under the law. Now the works of the flesh are plain: immorality, impurity, licentiousness, idolatry, sorcery, enmity, strife, jealousy, anger, selfishness, dissension, party spirit, envy, drunkenness, carousing, and the like. I warn you, as I warned you before, that those who do such things shall not inherit the kingdom of God. But the fruit of the Spirit is love, joy, peace, patience, kindness, goodness, faithfulness, gentleness, self-control; against such there is no law. And those who belong to Christ Jesus have crucified the flesh with its passions and desires.

If we live by the Spirit, let us also walk by the Spirit.
Let us have no self-conceit, no provoking of one another,
no envy of one another.

Galatians 5:13-26

So far, Paul had taught the Galatians about how and where to stand (5:1) and about running the race (5:7). Now it was time for them to learn about another form of upright posture: walking. To the first century mind, *walk* entailed the entire scope of a person's activities. A genuine Christian life is marked by a transformed walk; all that he does reveals a new power for living. As the inspirational preacher and author Andrew Murray said, "A man cannot live one hour a godly life except by the power of the Holy Ghost."

Jesus claimed to be "the way," which literally means "the road." The Christian life is a walk down the road of Christ under the Holy Spirit's direction. As Paul showed here, certain road marks (the fruit of the Spirit) assure the Christian that he is on the right path. And other not so nice road marks (works of the flesh) will reveal when he has strayed.

The Galatians were being confronted with two kinds of living: fleshly and spiritual. They had been called to freedom but were not to use their freedom as an opportunity for the flesh. Instead, they were to freely love one another (v. 13). The freedom to which Paul had pointed them may either be used or abused. It can best be put to use by loving others, but can be terribly abused by living fleshly lives.

By now we know that Scripture doesn't use the term "deny our flesh" with the concept of going on a diet. *Flesh* refers to evil desires. In this letter to the Galatians, the word was used to describe both Jewish sins (such as self-sufficient legalism) and Gentile sins (like immorality and witchcraft). In Paul's mind *flesh* denoted the heart of sin, the basic desire for evil.

Our freedom in Christ allows us to live new lives with loving relationships. Sadly enough, this is often not the case. As a prisoner's release is often just an opportunity to commit more crimes, so a Christian's freedom does not always mean a transformed lifestyle. Rather than yield himself to the life-giving, life-changing Spirit, he may still operate from his fleshly desires. And what is the result? War at two levels!

First, fleshly living causes war in the Body of Christ. The Galatians had the opportunity, through their new-found freedom, to truly love their brethren (v. 14). But because of divisive false teaching, they acted from their flesh and "took bites" out of one another (v. 15). Perhaps those who were "doctrinally right" found it particularly easy to nibble away on their heretical brothers.

A preacher once said that before he was saved, he found it easy to live in unity with others. Then, after becoming a Christian, everything changed. He found himself continually arguing with other believers. Why did relationship become so difficult? Because nothing had ever been as important to him as the Gospel, and he considered it very important to protect the truth. His goal was good, but his method was wrong.

Love must always be our motive in standing up for the truth. A lack of love disqualifies one from giving correction to a brother. It is ironic that in his desire to protect the Gospel, a "truth headhunter" often allows his relationships, the very heart of the Gospel, to suffer. If love does not govern his words, he's actually placed *his* doctrinal position before everything and everyone else.

Not only does fleshly living cause war in the Body of Christ, it also causes war in the body of a Christian. A battle takes place inside every Christian—the war between his flesh and the Holy Spirit for territorial control. Some Christians decide to fight the flesh with their own willpower, and this proves quite a mismatch.

During World War II, Japan conquered most of East Asia. The British, busy fighting in Europe, left their Crown Colony of Hong Kong with little military defense. A decision was made to send a few thousand Canadian troops, comprised mostly of untrained soldiers, to fight the tough Japanese Army. Of course, as everyone expected, most of the Canadians were killed. They had been sent on a suicide mission.

A Christian commits spiritual suicide by sending his relatively weak will to wage a war which only the Spirit can win. The message to the Galatians was clear: you are not strong enough to master your own flesh. Attempts at such foolish warfare will not only hinder your Christian walk but will even restrict your ability to walk.

Living the Christian life by rigid disciplines fails to deal with the major problem: selfish desires. The one who lives by principle rather than by the Spirit strives to conquer his fleshly desires through personal choices. We could compare this to a hospital patient dying from terminal cancer. Will he be cured by reading a book on preventative medicine and choosing to be well again? No, he will be saved only when his cancer is removed.

The Law (or principles) cannot change one's desires. Only the Holy Spirit's power is sufficient to gain victory over the flesh.

A new convert once tried feverishly to quit smoking. He felt that the habit was not a good testimony of Jesus to his friends. He tried to live by the unwritten rule that Christians shouldn't smoke, though the addiction was as strong as ever. Every evening, he would quit and trash his cigarettes, only to start up again the next morning. His desires proved far greater than his willpower.

One day, he realized he couldn't quit smoking until the Spirit changed his heart. He confessed his own inability and overpowering desires to God, and asked that these be changed by the Spirit's power. He threw away his cigarettes and never bought another pack. The Holy Spirit changed and empowered a weak Christian.

Paul went on to list some marks of fleshly living. These sins are all by-products of an untransformed heart. The Galatians were given this list to help them understand some of the things a Christian cannot overcome on his own. The sins may be divided into four categories:

- **Sexual sins,** including fornication, impurity, and licentiousness. These are Gentile sins which would typify the Galatian converts more than the circumcision party.

- **Doctrinal sins,** such as idolatry and sorcery. Remember that in this letter, Paul has drawn parallels between Jewish legalism and Gentile mystery religions. Both are man-made attempts at reaching God. These typify the sin of trusting anything other than Christ for one's righteousness.

- **Attitudinal or relational sins,** which are marked by several qualities. These include most of Paul's list: enmity, strife, jealousy, anger, selfishness, dissension, party spirit, and envy. The sins hit a bit close to the heart, as they are universal. For sure, all of Paul's readers have gotten the point: the flesh is not a pushover. Its wicked desires are active inside everyone.

- **Lifestyle sins,** such as drunkenness and carousing. These are probably to be understood as Gentile sins. Such loose living would have been relatively unheard of among Jews.

What were the Galatians to learn from such a barrage of negative words? Simply this: these are the marks of a person who lives by the flesh. And Paul's preaching had given them the only real answer for the problem of sin. Perhaps the circumcision party's disciplines had helped clean up some loose Gentile lifestyles. But certainly, the fleshly attitudes of sin would remain, merely covered over by external niceties. The Galatian believers were to see that a written set of rules was a poor battle weapon against such a formidable opponent.

Notice that Paul began his list by naming some sexual sins. Gentiles with carefree sexual lifestyles (like North America in the '70s and '80s) would have special trouble with these. Will a piece of paper that says, "Don't commit adultery" be enough to kill their desire? Well, maybe for a few days or weeks; maybe for a few months if they are especially disciplined. But the problem remained, buried under rules, and would inevitably rise to the surface.

Christians have made many strange attempts at conquering lust. A monk named Benedict of Nursia went outside on snowy days and rolled around in brambles. Another monk named Anthony put himself in a box and had it set in the middle of the desert. (He found this method didn't work very well when a young maiden brought him dinner.)

Today our "disciplines of self-control" lack such theatrics but are based on much the same mentality. Sooner or later, our flesh will be victorious if we are not absolutely dependent on the Spirit's power. The desire for unlawful sex will be far greater than a rule which says, "don't" and a will that says, "I won't." Power to resist and to change must come from elsewhere. The Psalmist discovered the source of his help. "I lift up my eyes to the hills. From whence does my help come? My help comes from the Lord, who made heaven and earth" (Ps. 121:1,2). God is the strength for holy living. He alone keeps us from doing the things we don't want to do (Rom. 7:19).

"Those who do such things shall not inherit the kingdom of God" (v. 21). Paul had warned them about this before (v. 21). He had done more than merely preach the philosophy of his "simple Gospel." Contrary to the thinking of some (including the circumcision party), he did not preach a "go-ahead-and-sin-that-grace-may-abound" type of message. He preached the automatic results of believing and receiving the simple Gospel. If a professed believer remains powerlessly unchanged with no results of right living, one may begin to doubt if he really came to grips with the Gospel. The outflow of the Gospel must starkly contrast his previous works of the flesh.

"But the fruit of the Spirit is love, joy, peace, patience, kindness, goodness, faithfulness, gentleness, self-control; against such there is no law" (vv. 22,23). These marks of discipleship are not received by reading a book. They are God-given qualities, new attitudes taking the place of old fleshly ones. (Compare these with Paul's list of attitude sins in verses 20 and 21.)

Notice that these are called "fruit" of the Spirit, as opposed to "works" of the flesh (v. 19). Have you ever sat for hours, watching fruit grow? (If you have, you probably aren't a whole lot of fun to be with.) Fruit just hangs as part of the tree, growing slowly and naturally. Apple blossoms seldom grit their petals and confess, "I'm going to be an apple, I'm going to be an apple...." They become apples because they are part of an apple tree. What a contrast to legalists, those who work and work and work, trying to live acceptable Christian lives. They try their best to produce acceptable fruit, only to find it filled with rottenness and worms. The works of the flesh are dead works (Heb. 6:1) stemming from dead trees.

This passage closes with two essential marks of a Christian: the Cross and the Spirit. These signify the death and life of a believer. His flesh has been put to death at the Cross. Only then could he be made alive by the Spirit. "Those who belong to Christ Jesus have crucified the flesh with its passions and desires" (v. 24). Notice the past tense, "have crucified." Christians don't come together for "crucifixion parties" to put these awful desires to death. When Christ died, we died with Him. The attractions of this world are garbage (or "dung," as Paul prefers to call them) in light of the crucified Christ. Passions and desires are dealt with only at the Cross of Christ, not through self-invented crucifixion ceremonies (like the ones our monk friends put themselves through).

The Christian life begins at the Cross. And throughout this life of "Spirit vs. flesh" warfare, the battle must be fought at the foot of the Cross. This means a Christian must daily remember that his only reason for living is in the fact that Jesus died for him. The believer who moves past the Cross of Christ is the one who finds other ways of fighting the battle. The successful Christian soldier is first and foremost dead to his flesh. But just as important, he is made alive by the Spirit.

"If we live by the Spirit, let us also walk by the Spirit" (v. 25). As we were dead before the Spirit gave us life, so now we are lame if we don't continually depend on the Spirit's life. A dead man can do nothing to make himself alive, and a lame man is completely unable to make himself walk. The Spirit of God enables us to live the Christian life; we cannot do so with our own strength.

By embracing the Law, the Galatians neglected the Holy Spirit, their only power for living the Christian life. This type of "living by the Spirit" would result in a loss of self-conceit and would provide healthy relationships within the church (v. 25). Such supernatural living removes the threat of pride. After all, can a nice apple be proud of the fact that it turned out red and juicy?

God receives the glory for a successful Christian life. He makes alive; His Spirit produces fruit. He alone gives us the power to walk in a manner worthy of our calling.

Questions, Review, and Interpretation

1. What would it mean for the Galatian believers to stand fast in their freedom?

2. What does it mean to "wait for the hope of righteousness"?

3. How would one use his freedom as "an opportunity for the flesh"?

4. What does the term *flesh* mean?

5. Why would the Galatians not know the power of the Holy Spirit?

Application:

1. How do you "stand fast" in your freedom?

2. How does waiting for the hope of righteousness affect you now?

3. With what secondary issues (like circumcision) do believers in our day require Christians to be identified?

4. How has the Spirit conquered your flesh? What are some areas with which you presently struggle?

15

Burden Bearers

Brethren, if a man is overtaken in any trespass, you who are spiritual should restore him in a spirit of gentleness. Look to yourself, lest you too be tempted. Bear one another's burdens, and so fulfil the law of Christ. For if any one thinks he is something, when he is nothing, he deceives himself. But let each one test his own work, and then his reason to boast will be in himself alone and not in his neighbor. For each man will have to bear his own load.

Let him who is taught the word share all good things with him who teaches.

Do not be deceived; God is not mocked, for whatever a man sows, that he will also reap. For he who sows to his own flesh will from the flesh reap corruption; but he who sows to the Spirit will from the Spirit reap eternal life. And let us not grow weary in well-doing, for in due season we shall reap, if we do not lose heart. So then, as we have opportunity, let us do good to all men, and especially to those who are of the household of faith.

Galatians 6:1-10

Camels are of great value to various groups of people in the world. These strange creatures can travel quickly through waterless, dusty deserts where other pack animals would fade with thirst and hunger. The camel asks for little in return for its hard work. It can live for days with no food or water, surviving from nourishment stored in its own hump. And most importantly, this burden-bearer can carry about 400 pounds as well as its rider (provided the rider doesn't weigh 400 pounds, too)!

As unflattering as it may sound, we can study this passage by picturing the believer as a "spiritual camel." A Christian "burden bearer" can carry the weight of his brother's problem, and he also asks for nothing in return. Paul was asking the Galatians to become true burden bearers and be of great value to needy brothers and sisters. This is the most practical section in Paul's entire letter. But these instructions are not to be removed from previous chapters. The practice of a Christian, his daily walk, is merely an outflow of the grace poured into his life by God.

In the last chapter, Paul gave a lesson on fruit growing. Actions and attitudes of a Christian were seen to be a product of the Holy Spirit's indwelling life. Now the fruit becomes more specific, affecting actual relationships. Paul chooses to restrict his lesson on relationships to two aspects: restoring a backslidden brother and giving to others. Both of these would have been of concern to the Galatians, sheep under the attack of ravenous wolves.

How to Restore a Backslidden Brother (6:1-5)

A Christian's attitude toward a backslidden brother should be a reflection of Jesus. Before we study this attitude, however, it's important to note the way in which Paul describes both the backslider and the one who brings restoration. The backslider is one "overtaken in any trespass" (v. 1). Remember the "race" analogy from the previous chapter (5:7), in which we learned how easy it is for the runner to stray? In this chapter we find an example of one who has strayed from the path by failing to keep his eyes on Jesus, the goal. How had he strayed? Paul didn't really say, but taken in context of the whole book, we may assume that he had become involved in legalism. Perhaps he had believed the circumcision party's message and had begun to base his Christian life on the Law rather than on Jesus. This was true backsliding.

On the other hand, perhaps he was a brother who had become involved in types of sins mentioned in chapter five as "works of the flesh." If that was the case, the "spiritual" brother was now called on to respond in a way that the legalist wouldn't. He hated sin every bit as much as the pious Jew, but his response to the sinner would be quite different. The legalist would condemn rather than restore. The one who has received God's undeserved grace will shower such grace on others. Chuck Girard eloquently warns the Church when he sings, "Don't shoot your wounded."

The "restoring brother" is supposed to be "spiritual" (v. 1). We often use the term *spiritual* facetiously when describing stuff-shirted pride. Actually, the word *spiritual* describes one who lives by the Spirit, as opposed to the "carnal" brother who lives by the flesh. The spiritual brother is marked by the fruit of the Spirit, just as clearly as an apple tree is marked by apples.

Paul mentioned five ways that a spiritual brother should seek to restore a fallen brother:

With gentleness

Remember that gentleness is a fruit of the Spirit. Moreover, James tells us that gentleness is a mark of wisdom (James 3:17). The one who deals gently with a backslidden brother may be considered wise and Spirit-filled. Harsh condemnation, the opposite of gentle restoration, may therefore be seen as unwise and fleshly.

The backslidden believer is like a baby learning to walk. His parents would be all "goo-goo-eyed and excited," giving the child gentle encouragement to take those first steps. When he falls, they set him back on his feet to try again. No parent would scream at their stumbling infant, calling him "incompetent and weak" or give him a swift kick each time he fell.

The Christian who struggles with sin is to be treated in the same way. You, the spiritual brother or sister, must come to him with all the gentleness shown to you by Jesus. "Come to me, all who labor...for I am gentle and lowly in heart..." (Matt. 11:28,29).

With empathy

"Look to yourself, lest you too be tempted" (v. 1). Empathy is a trait which helps one understand and feel for someone else's situation. We are not to view the sinner as part of some circus freak show, weird and cast off because of his sin. We are to see the sinner as one who fell to the enemy; the enemy who could have conquered any one of us. The circumcision party, proud of their own Law-keeping disciplines, would be unable to share such empathy with a sinner. To them, the sinner was someone who just wasn't good enough. A legalist is like a harsh coach who quickly cuts the poor player rather than help him improve his game.

Empathy does more than allow us to feel for others. It also keeps our eyes open to our own weaknesses apart from God. Recognizing our weaknesses strengthens us, because our hope is placed in a far greater Strength.

With identification

We Christians have a unique way of gossiping. It usually begins with, "Let's pray for so and so. Did you know that she...." The "concerned intercessor" then goes on to describe the gory details of someone else's sin, showing all the "empathy" and "gentleness" his voice can muster. Restoration of a backslidden brother usually requires more than distant prayer. The spiritual brother will identify with his fallen friend. That doesn't mean he goes *with* him and copies his sin, but he does go *to* the sinner to bear his burden through listening and caring.

The Jews of Jesus' day couldn't understand how a public religious teacher could relate to sinners. In the same way, the circumcision party stood far off and condemned the sinner, while the spiritual brother drew near to help him.

Christians may view an AIDS victim with the attitude of, "You've made your bed, now lie in it." Or else we may show mock concern for the burdened sinner with, "Gee, that's a heavy load. I'll pray for you." The spiritual brother goes farther by saying, "Let me help you carry it." He reaches out, physically draws near, and picks up the fallen believer.

With humility

"If any one thinks he is something, when he is nothing, he deceives himself" (v. 3). Legalism results in spiritual pride. The circumcision party loved to glory in the flesh (6:13). They found pleasure in external marks of religion, in the fact that others viewed them as "giants of the faith." Such pride would remove them from a weak believer struggling with sin. He would be viewed by such "spiritual giants" as a "spiritual midget."

The truly spiritual Christian is not deceived by his own external markings of faith. He knows that his success, his pure life, is only a result of God's grace. Such humility allows him to relate to a backslidden brother as an equal.

In another letter, Paul asks the Philippians to count others as better than themselves (Phil. 2:3). In a letter to Timothy, Paul the great apostle confesses that he is the "foremost of sinners" (I Tim. 1:15). Such humility allowed him to reach out to anyone who needed God, be it a runaway slave like Onesimus or the prison guards who would later hold him captive.

With impartiality

"Let each one test his own work, and then his reason to boast will be in himself alone and not in his neighbor. For each man will have to bear his own load" (vv. 4,5). False teaching had brought division to the Galatian church. Paul had warned them that "a party spirit" and "dissension" are works of the flesh. (*Party spirit* could also be translated "divisive spirit.")

He was writing to people divided by a minor issue—circumcision—and had lost sight of their faith's central issue—Jesus. They had probably begun to form their own little cliques. Rather than share God's attitude of accepting the backslidden brother, sin and all, they would have placed other demands on him. He would be accepted into their fellowship only after he met the group standards. The fallen Christian was treated like a skid-row bum, devoid of circumcision party etiquette, unacceptable to the church's high standards.

The spiritual Christian was asked to examine himself rather than the group. Attempts would then be made to draw the backslider back into a spiritual walk, not into a social club. Restoration was made first between the brother and God, and then the same restoration was extended to the church body. The fleshly circumcision party would have lacked all these attitudes. The truly spiritual Galatians, those bearing the fruit of the Spirit, would prove their spirituality by sharing such attitudes for needy brethren.

Lessons on Giving (6:6-10)

The second main lesson from this passage seems quite out of place in the Epistle. Why would Paul teach about giving after dealing with legalism for five chapters? It may be possible that those verses do not all relate to "giving," but for now we will assume they do.

The Galatians had become misdirected in their giving. Remember who wanted to make much of them for no good purpose (4:17)? The circumcision party looked for a nice reward for delivering heresy. And the Galatians gave it to them. By giving to false teachers, they actually identified with false teaching.

Paul's instructions about financial giving can be seen as answering three questions:

To whom should we give?

Martin Luther cringed at the thought of commenting on this passage, because he saw sickening abuses by the rich clergy of his day. Honest church pastors and missionaries sometimes feel the same way today. Financial abuses by some prosperous church leaders cast a very evil shadow on the honest Bible teacher. Still, the teacher does deserve payment for his work, though he usually doesn't expect it. Just because the circumcision party abused this privilege (though they didn't even deserve it) does not mean the faithful teacher should lose his privilege.

The Bible calls Christians to give to the one who teaches them, stating that "the laborer deserves his wages" (Luke 10:7). Paul does not nullify the practice of paying a Bible teacher. He redirects their giving away from the circumcision party to honest, worthy teachers. By giving to false teachers, the Galatians sowed to their own flesh (v. 8). They gave to a program that worked against them, not to mention that it stood in opposition to the Spirit of God.

Why should we give?

Sowing and reaping is seen by some as a natural law, like gravity. We throw an apple up in the air, and gravity causes it to fall to the ground and bruise itself. We give $50 to a preacher on television, and we'll get $500 in return. Or we commit a sin now, and it will haunt us for the rest of our lives.

The context of sowing and reaping for this passage is "giving money." But it also relates to the concepts of chapter five: the war between the flesh and the Spirit. We have already commented that "sowing to the flesh" meant that the Galatians were giving to the circumcision party. Sowing and reaping differs from an impersonal, natural law, because a personal God is directly involved. That's why the "give $50, take $500" mentality is wrong. Though God's name may be used, such a concept reduces Him to a formula.

God does promise certain consequences for a person's actions. Deuteronomy 27 and 28 list some curses and blessings for the Israelites' disobedience or obedience. They didn't have God on a leash, making Him turn whichever way their actions dictated, but they could expect Him to respond to their sin as well as to their righteousness. Unfortunately, history shows that they sowed to their flesh and reaped judgment.

By giving to a program opposed to the Spirit, the Galatians also sowed to their flesh. They could not expect God to honor such misdirected generosity. Instead, they would reap corruption (or destruction, as the New International Version descriptively translates).

But God will honor the one who "sows to the Spirit," which in this passage refers to the one who gives to a valid "spiritual" teacher. His giving may not be shouted by such flaunting flesh-lovers as the circumcision party, but God sees their action just as clearly as Jesus saw the widow give her few coins. They will reap eternal benefits.

How should we give?

"And let us not grow weary in well-doing, for in due season we shall reap, if we do not lose heart" (v. 9). This explains the focus which a Christian giver should have. His eyes are not on the juicy "hundredfold reward" or on the return of the "bread cast upon the water." He doesn't stop giving when he fails to get back as much as he gave away. The point is, the believer is marked by an attitude of tireless giving, in spite of external blessings (or lack of them). His eyes are on God to repay him in His own time and way.

This entire lesson on giving is overshadowed and underscored by verse ten. "So then, as we have opportunity, let us do good to all men, and especially to those who are of the household of faith." A Spirit-inspired Christian cares for everyone, giving to needy people whether or not they are redeemed. At the same time, he does hold a special place in his heart for the needy brother.

The lifestyle of a man inspired by the Spirit differs greatly from that of one driven by the flesh. Each group treats people differently and may expect opposite rewards. But the greatest difference is the most basic. Flesh-driven Christians are concerned with programs, rules, or themselves, while Spirit-inspired Christians are ultimately concerned with one earthly thing: other people.

Part Six

Conclusion:
The Ultimate Act of Grace

16

Large Letters for the Cross

See with what large letters I am writing to you with my own hand. It is those who want to make a good showing in the flesh that would compel you to be circumcised, and only in order that they may not be persecuted for the cross of Christ. For even those who receive circumcision do not themselves keep the law, but they desire to have you circumcised that they may glory in your flesh. But far be it from me to glory except in the cross of our Lord Jesus Christ, by which the world has been crucified to me, and I to the world. For neither circumcision counts for anything, nor uncircumcision, but a new creation. Peace and mercy be upon all who walk by this rule, upon the Israel of God.

Henceforth let no man trouble me; for I bear on my body the marks of Jesus.

The grace of our Lord Jesus Christ be with your spirit, brethren. Amen.

Galatians 6:11-18

A dramatic preacher can really make church interesting. He usually begins his sermons in a rather soft-spoken manner, but by the time he's reached the peak of his message, all caution is thrown to the wind. His volume increases by several decibels and his arms flail in every direction; the main point is being brought home with all the fury he can muster.

Paul closed his letter dramatically with large letters, written by his own hand. (The rest of the epistle was probably dictated to a secretary.) He signed most of his letters personally, each time using some distinguishable trademark. Here he used large letters for the Cross of Christ. Paul's large letters made some concluding statements.

Each of these statements highlight and summarize his message to the Galatians: circumcision is useless, and only the Cross is of central importance to the faith. These large letters are like the final credits run across the screen at a movie's end. The Cross was the reason for the message of the letter; the work of Christ got full credit for the successful Christian life. If the Galatians saw nothing else, they were to clearly see the Cross of Christ in these final words.

We can divide Paul's concluding words into four basic statements, two about circumcision and two about the Cross.

Circumcision is performed in order to please people.

"It is those who want to make a good showing in the flesh that would compel you to be circumcised, and only in order that they may not be persecuted for the cross of Christ" (v. 12). The circumcision party played the "numbers game." The more people who were circumcised, the better they'd look. Their motive was to please people.

Churches and mission organizations can sometimes fall into this trap. We should always examine our hearts to be sure we're not trying to build up "empires" in order to "make a good showing in the flesh." Circumcision-party mentality will place the results above the means. The faithful believer will place the means (that is, the Cross) above results in numbers. Whenever we become consumed with "multiplication in ministry" for the sake of a good showing (or for a good newsletter to supporters), it would be good to remember the simple insight of a wise old preacher: "Jesus began with twelve disciples, and died with only eleven."

Circumcision kept persecutors at bay, serving as an outward symbol of conformity to an acceptable religion. The Galatians had been set apart by the Cross, but because of circumcision—the new standard they had adopted—they could no longer sing, "The world behind me, the Cross before me." Their heart's message would be, "Now that the Cross is behind me, the whole world is before me." Instead of "Though none go with me, still I will follow," they would sing, "As I follow, I can take everyone with me." External religion frees the sincere believer from the persecution promised by the One on the Cross.

Circumcision is based in hypocritical pride.

"For even those who receive circumcision do not themselves keep the law, but they desire to have you circumcised that they may glory in your flesh" (v. 13). People of the world find hypocrisy in Christians very unappealing. You may have talked with someone who won't step foot in church because the smell of hypocrisy is too great. Seeing so much hypocritical pride in their own world of sin, people look for something better in Christians. The widely publicized "money scandals" of church leaders show that the world expects honesty and integrity from the Church.

Unfortunately, the circumcision party offered their own walk of pride to their audience in the form of external religion. To them, circumcision should be the standard for church membership. New converts would feel quite pleased with themselves for being able to handle this initiation rite, and the circumcision party would be especially pleased over increased numbers.

External forms of religion tend to feed the pride that the Cross promises to kill. The one who emphasizes only the outward marks of the faith—Bible reading, prayer schedules, programs—may well be acting from a proud, unchanged heart. Sooner or later, that hidden heart of pride will surface.

The Cross leads one to relinquish all worldly ambitions.

"But far be it from me to glory except in the cross of our Lord Jesus Christ, by which the world has been crucified to me, and I to the world" (v. 14). Paul separated himself from the circumcision party with the word *but*. They may glory in some external forms of religion, but Paul gloried in the Cross alone, the entire point of his religion.

With such a concern for fleshly rituals and legalistic principles, the circumcision party found hope in a "Jesus + ___" formula. Such a formula would not have worked for Paul. For the apostle, all formulas for living had ended with Jesus, and a new life had begun through Jesus alone.

For Paul, the Cross of Christ overshadowed the present life. Worldly things, so intriguing to worldly people, became as money to a dead man—absolutely useless. Notice that Paul didn't say, "I boast in uncircumcision." For him, such a basis of pride would have been equally meaningless. He had no grounds to boast in what he did or didn't do, for his single hope was in the Cross of Christ.

A gifted Bible teacher once went through a time of relinquishing her ministry. When invited to speak somewhere, she declined by saying, "I really don't know anything at the moment but Christ and Him crucified, and it wouldn't take very long to say that."

Do our Christian lives speak louder than the Cross? If so, we need to quieten our outward show of religion, our glorying in the flesh. Only then will people hear the message of the Cross of Christ shouting loudly through our lives.

The Cross has created something new.

"For neither circumcision counts for anything, nor uncircumcision, but a new creation" (v. 15). This is the entire point of Galatians: fleshly activities (or "works") cannot make spiritual people. Only at the Cross of Christ is someone made new.

Through the Cross, God ushered in an entirely new age. (Not the "new age" referred to by twentieth-century mystics.) God is in the process of doing more than making a few people "new creatures." He is at work in the cosmos, bringing in an entirely new creation, of which we are a part. We are people of God's colossal "Cosmos Project" put in effect at the Cross of Christ. The "Israel of God" (v. 16) is part of God's reorganizing scheme in the "Cosmos Project."

As children of promise, supernaturally born through the work of Jesus, we are now spiritual "Jews." As Paul mentions in Ephesians, we are part of the "commonwealth of Israel." The Galatians didn't need to bother with outdated rites to become part of the Jewish faith, because it is through Jesus that they are considered true Jews, made into covenant people by God's gracious work. What a fitting final blow to the circumcision party! Paul's final "knockdown punch" turns *them* into the "Gentile sinners." The true Israel of God will place their confidence in God alone, not in their own activities.

So people of God are branded by the Cross. Paul bore on his body the marks of Jesus (v. 17) in stark contrast to the marks of circumcision. The circumcision party bore marks that identified them with fleshly rituals, while Paul's marks identified him with the Cross of Christ.

What are these marks? They probably refer to scars which resulted from persecution. It is interesting that as

Jesus bore marks from the cross on his hands, side, and feet, so Paul is scarred in his battle for the Cross. The word *mark* is used in Greek literature as a brand that would identify a certain slave with his master. Today the same idea is used in branding cattle. Paul saw the bruises, scars, and gashes left on his body as that which identified him with his master, Jesus.

Paul closed this letter in the same way that he began it: grace. The grace of Jesus is well worth fighting and suffering for. Only that grace of God, given through Christ, provides sufficient reason and power for living. By grace the Galatians had entered the Kingdom; and by grace they will endure until the Kingdom is completely established.

Questions, Review, and Interpretation

1. What does it mean to restore a fallen brother "in a spirit of gentleness"?

2. How does one "sow to his flesh"? What is the result of doing this?

3. Why does Paul write in large letters at the end of this epistle?

4. What is the basic difference between circumcision and the Cross?

5. Why does Paul use the term *the Israel of God*? What would this term mean to the Galatians?

Application:

1. Imagine that a Christian friend has backslidden and is slandering you. How will you act toward him?

2. How would you apply Paul's exhortation on giving in Galatians chapter six?

3. Which is more obvious in your life: the Cross of Christ or the mentality of circumcision?

4. What are some specific ways that the Cross of Christ has marked your life?

5. Why do you need the grace of God?

Appendix

Thirty Minutes a Day

30 Minutes of Bible Study Each Day

Decide on a book of the Bible that you want to study for one month. Before you begin, purchase a folder to store all your insights from your study, and write down all that you know about the book that you plan to study.

Day 1

Read the book through in one sitting, rapidly, aloud.

Day 2

Read the book through again, and write down the *big idea* of the book.

Day 3

Read the book through again, looking for repeated words or phrases. Write down these words or phrases, then ask why the author uses them. Record your answers.

Day 4

Ask *who*. Write down all the people mentioned. Which ones are the main characters? Who are these people? Why are they important? Are they mentioned anywhere else in the Bible? Check your concordance. What have you learned about these people? Summarize your thoughts.

Day 5

Ask *where*. List the geographical locations. Which ones are important in understanding this book? Find these locations on a map. If they are cities, pick one or two and read about them in a Bible dictionary. If they are countries, choose one or two and read about them in a Bible dictionary. Think about how this information helps you understand the book. Write down your ideas.

Day 6

Ask *when*. Look for words that indicate time: *before, after, while, during, then, no longer, as long as*, etc. This should help you see the sequence of events. What happened in the past? What is taking place presently? What are future events?

Day 7

Ask *what*. What events are taking place in this book? What topics are discussed? Write down your answers.

Day 8

Observe and record contrasts. These can be broad contrasts, such as two contrasting characters, contrasting events, or contrasting themes. They can be less broad, being contrasts within a paragraph and identified by the conjunction, *but*.

Day 9

What illustrations does the author use? Are they from everyday life situations, from Scripture, from past history, or from personal experiences?

Day 10

Write down any words or terms that you don't understand. Go through the following steps to discover what these terms or words mean:

1. How is the word or phrase used in this book? Write down anything you learn from its use in each passage. Consider the context of the passage. What is this passage talking about? How does the main idea of this passage help you understand this word or phrase? Consider this for every passage where the word is used in the book you are studying.

2. How does the author use the same word or phrase in other books? Use a concordance to help you find this information.

3. Look the word up in a concordance, and check the original Greek or Hebrew. (The introduction to the concordance will tell you how to do such exercises.)

4. If you have a word-study book, look the word up in that book.

5. Look up the passage in a commentary, and see if anything is mentioned about the word or phrase.

6. Ask someone else for their insights.

7. Look up the word in your native-language dictionary.

8. Read the passage in another translation.

9. Formulate your definition of the word or phrase, then insert it into the passage to see if it makes sense. Do you now understand the passage?

Day 11

Do the same as Day 10. Finish the work for Day 10, or find the meaning for another word or term.

Day 12

If the book is six chapters or less, write a brief summary of each paragraph. If the book is more than six chapters, then write a brief chapter summary.

Day 13

Think through each paragraph and ask this question: How does each paragraph lead into the next? Does the following paragraph continue on the same topic or does it change topics, characters, ideas, or events. How does the paragraph fit with the overall message, the *big idea* of the book?

Can you discover how the author has organized his material? How is the material organized: biographically, geographically, chronologically, logically, or thematically?

Does the author answer a series of questions? Does he move from a problem to the solution, from general to specifics, from theology to practical application? (If you are working with a book with more than six chapters, you may want to go chapter by chapter for Day 13.)

Day 14

Continue working through Day 13.

Day 15

Again, continue working through Day 13.

Day 16

Consider historical background. How did the original audience receive and understand this book?

1. If the book is a letter to a church, answer the following questions:

a. When was the church founded? Can you find any information in the book of Acts? Consult a Bible dictionary.

b. Who founded the church? What kind of reception did these original evangelists receive?

c. Read through the letter and discover the church's strengths and weaknesses.

d. Imagine what it would be like to be a member of this church.

e. What is the prevailing religion in the area? What religious beliefs did these Christians have prior to their conversion?

f. Are there any customs or cultural insights that would be helpful to know? Do some reading in outside sources.

2. If the book is a historical narrative:

a. What was happening in Israel's (or the Early Church's) history before and after this book?

b. What was happening in the surrounding cultures?

c. How does this book fit into the overall history of God's people?

3. If the book is one of the Prophets:

a. When did this prophet minister?

b. What was going on in Israel's history at that time?

c. Who received the prophecy?

Day 17

Continue working on Day 16.

Day 18

Ask the literary question: What type of literature is being used in the whole book, or the passage under consideration?

The first distinction is to determine whether the passage is prose or poetry. Poetry uses figures of speech and is not to be interpreted literally. Learn to recognize the following types of literature. Read about them in a Bible dictionary or reference book. Understand their specific characteristics so you interpret correctly.

1. Epistles: the New Testament letter form; composed of various parts

2. Gospels

3. Parables

4. Oracles: found in the Prophets

5. Didactic literature: having the purpose of teaching

6. Apocalyptic literature. Examples: Revelation, parts of Isaiah, Ezekiel, Daniel, and Zechariah

7. Historical narratives: literature which traces the history of Israel or the Church

8. Wisdom literature: found in Proverbs and Ecclesiastes. It is also very important for you to read up on Hebrew poetry so you can understand the Psalms and the Prophets.

Day 19

Meditate on either the whole book or a certain passage. Just spend today thinking about the book. Write down your insights.

Day 20

Finish anything you haven't completed, or decide for yourself what study you want to do today.

Day 21

Observe progression. Does the author move to a climax of ideas, emotion, or story line? Does he move from specific to general? From a question to the answer? From a statement to an illustration? From teaching to application? Observe and record your insights and then ask: Why?

Day 22

Wrestle with a difficult passage. Read through the passage several times. Meditate on the passage. Bombard the passage with *why* questions. Answer the *why* questions that you asked. Consider the context and main ideas of the surrounding paragraphs. How does this difficult passage fit in to the overall message of the book? Write down your conclusions and ask yourself if this is a reasonable interpretation. Does it go against any major truth or teaching of the Bible? Ask someone else their opinion of this passage.

Day 23

Discover the author's main concern. What does he want the readers to know and understand? What are the readers' main concerns? Have they asked certain questions that the author is answering? Write down what you discover.

Day 24

Read the whole book through again in one sitting. Think once again about the overall message of the book.

Day 25

Bombard the text with *why* questions. Write out your questions, then try to answer them. Is the answer found somewhere in the book? Just sit back and think for a while; sometimes the answer just involves allowing yourself time to think. Be sure to write down your answers; don't consider them unimportant. Share your ideas with someone else.

Day 26

Do the same thing you did for Day 25.

Day 27

Summarize the basic truths of this book. Ask yourself how these truths apply to your life in the twentieth century. Does the book:

1. Teach me something I didn't know?

2. Bring correction?

3. Bring encouragement?

4. Help me understand more about God or mankind?

Day 28

In light of these truths (what you wrote for Day 27), ask "What changes need to take place in my life? Am I to change what I believe? Am I to change in my relationships with others? Am I to change in my relationship with God?" Try and personalize the book into your life. Write down your answers.

Day 29

What truths or applications could you make from this book if you were teaching it? Write them out.

Day 30

Pray through the application process. Write out your prayer as a permanent record of your application.

Review what you wrote about the book before you began your study, and be encouraged with your progress. File all your questions and answers in a file. Now...decide what book you will study next.

Instructions for Continuing Bible Study

You can adapt this program to the time available. You could reduce the time you spend each day to 20 minutes, or increase it to whatever time is available for Bible study.

It is best to make Bible study a daily event. Some days will be more productive than others, but keep moving through the program day by day. This will develop a habit of daily Bible study. Be sure to do this only to know Christ better, not to try to please Him.

What if you are studying a large book? We would suggest that you do smaller books for the first few months. When you want to try a larger book, then you may adapt the program. Take Day 1, and instead of doing the assigned task for one day, do it for two days. Do the same for Day 2, Day 3, and so on all the way through the daily assignments. Thus it will take you two months to finish the book instead of one month. If the book is extremely long, you may adapt the program so that you spend 3 or 4 days on each assignment. Then the book will take three or four months to complete.